Book 1

Just Vocabulary

Elementary

Includes Answer Key

Carol Lethaby
Ana Acevedo
Jeremy Harmer

Viva Books

New Delhi | Mumbai | Chennai | Kolkata | Bangalore | Hyderabad | Kochi | Guwahati

Photo acknowledgements

p.9 a ©Robbie Jack/Corbis, b ©Corbis, c ©Daniel Bosler/Photographer's Choice/Getty Images, d ©Holly Harris/Stone +/Getty Images, e ©Ghislain & Marie David de Lossy/The Image Bank/Getty Images, f ©David Hoffman Photo Library/Alamy, g ©Corbis, h ©Yellow Dog Productions/The Image Bank/Getty Images, I ©Jeff Cadge/Photographer's Choice/Getty Images, j ©Jacques Langevin/Corbis Sygma, k ©Dynamic Graphics Group/Creatas/Alamy, l ©Bigshots/The Image Bank/Getty Images; p.10 tl ©Simon Marcus/Corbis, tc ©Jeff Speed/First Light/Getty Images, tr ©Corbis, b ©Bill Varie/Corbis; p.17 tl ©Steve Smith/Taxi/Getty Images, tc ©Bill Hickey/The Image Bank/Getty Images, tr ©Dirk Anschutz/Photonica/Getty Images, bl ©Stefano Oppo/Photonica/Getty Images, br ©Karl Weatherly/Photographer's Choice/Getty Images; p.18 tl ©Lawrence Manning/Corbis, bl ©Adrian Wilson/Beateworks/Corbis, tr ©Moodboard/Corbis, cr ©Simon Jarratt/Corbis, br ©Hubert Boesl/dpa/Corbis; p.24 t l-r ©Daniel Smith/Stone/Getty Images, ©George Tiedemann/New Sport/Corbis, ©Ryan McVay/Stone +/Getty Images, ©Purestock/Alamy, ©John Lamb/Photonica/Getty Images, ©John Kelly/Iconica/Getty Images, ©Ace Stock Limted/Alamy, ©John Rowley/Stone/Getty Images, ©Aflo Foto Agency/Alamy, ©Geoff A Howard/Alamy; p.27, ©Stockdisc Premium/Alamy; p.34 1 ©Peter Cade/Stone/Getty Images, 2 ©Steve Chenn/Corbis, 3 ©geogphotos/Alamy, 4 ©Christa Stadtler/Photofusion Picture Library/Alamy, 5 ©Werner Otto/Alamy, 6 ©Pawel Libera/Corbis, 7 ©David Churchill/Arcaid/Alamy, 8 ©Ross Nicholas/Phoenix Photos, 9 ©Stockbyte Gold/Alamy, 10 ©Ross Nicholas/Phoenix Photos, 11 ©Ross Nicholas/Phoenix Photos, 12 ©David Batterbury/Eye Ubiquitous/Corbis, 13 ©Frank Chmura/Alamy, 14 ©Ediface/Corbis; p.37 a ©Ablestock/Hemera Technologies/Alamy, b ©I. Glory/Alamy, c ©PhotoSpin, Inc/Alamy, d ©Stockbyte Silver/Alamy, e ©PhotoSpin, Inc/Alamy, f ©PhotoSpin, Inc/Alamy, g ©Stockbyte Silver/Alamy, Mozart ©The Art Archive/Corbis, Coldplay ©Stephane Cardinale/People Avenue/Corbis, Eminem ©Reuters/Corbis, Armstrong ©Bettmann/Corbis, Cash ©Neal Preston/Corbis, Anastacia ©Susana Vera/Reuters/Corbis; p.38 a ©Lesley Sandles/Alamy, b ©KPA/CBI/Sven Hoogerhuis/Content Mine International/Alamy, c ©M J Kim/Reportage/Getty Images, d ©Craig Lovell/Eagle Visions Photography/Alamy; p.41 a, c, d ©Ross Nicholas/Phoenix Photos; p.86 a ©Purestock/Alamy, b ©Arco Images/Alamy, c ©Andrew Darrington/Alam, d ©John Foxx/Alamy, e ©Purestock/Alamy, f ©Purestock/Alamy, g ©David Hoskings/Alamy, h ©Tim Graham/Alamy, I ©Goodshoot/Corbis, j ©Ivan Vdovin/JAI/Corbis, k ©DLILLC/Corbis, l ©George Logan/zefa/Corbis; p.52 ©Jeremy Horner/Corbis; p.57 a ©Peter Aprahamian/Corbis, b ©Philip Brown/Corbis, c ©Guido Manuilo/EPA/Corbis, d ©Patrick Ward/Corbis, e ©Tom Sibley/Corbis, f ©Kathy Collins/Corbis, g ©Richard Southall/Arcaid/Corbis, h ©Ediface/Corbis

First Indian Edition 2009

VIVA BOOKS PRIVATE LIMITED

- 4737/23 Ansari Road, Daryaganj, New Delhi 110 002
  E-mail: vivadelhi@vivagroupindia.net, Tel. 42242200
- 76, Service Industries, Shirvane, Sector 1, Nerul, Navi Mumbai 400 706
  E-mail: vivamumbai@vivagroupindia.net, Tel. 27721273, 27721274
- Jamals Fazal Chambers, 26 Greams Road, Chennai 600 006
  E-mail: vivachennai@vivagroupindia.net, Tel. 28290304, 28294241
- B-103, Jindal Towers, 21/1A/3 Darga Road, Kolkata 700 017
  E-mail: vivakolkata@vivagroupindia.net, Tel. 22836381, 22816713
- 7, Sovereign Park Apartments, 56-58, K. R. Road, Basavanagudi, Bangalore 560 004
  E-mail: vivabangalore@vivagroupindia.net, Tel. 26607409, 26607410
- 101-102 Mughal Marc Apartments, 3-4-637 to 641, Narayanguda, Hyderabad 500 029
  E-mail: vivahyderabad@vivagroupindia.net, Tel. 27564481, 27564482
- First Floor, Beevi Towers, SRM Road, Kaloor, Kochi 682 018, Kerala
  E-mail: vivakochi@vivagroupindia.net, Tel: 0484-2403055, 2403056
- H. No. 12, P. B. Road, Near Arya Hospital, Rehabari, Guwahati 781 008
  E-mail: vivaguwahati@vivagroupindia.net, Tel: 0361-2735624

www.vivagroupindia.com

Published by arrangement with

Marshall Cavendish Education
119 Wardour Street
London W1F 0OW, UK

ISBN-10: 81-309-1110-8
ISBN-13: 978-81-309-1110-6

Published by Vinod Vasishtha for Viva Books Private Limited, 4737/23, Ansari Road, Daryaganj, New Delhi - 110 002. Printed and bound by Raj Press, R-3, Inderpuri, New Delhi - 110 012.

Contents

Introduction

For the student

Welcome to *Just Vocabulary*. You can use this book with other students and a teacher, or you can work alone with it.

In this book you will find 24 units. Each unit has a section on useful vocabulary (with pictures, texts and explanations) and a section on language 'functions' (that means conversational English for use in many different situations).

There is an accompanying CD to help you with the many dialogues in the book. Where you see the symbol it means that you can listen to the CD. You will also find an Audioscript at the back of the book which contains all the recordings on the CD.

When you see this symbol ( ) it means that the answers to the practice exercises are in the Answer Key at the back of the book. You can check your answers there.

We hope that this book helps you progress in English, and, above all, that you enjoy using it.

For the teacher

This book is part of a series designed to be used alone or to supplement any course book you may be using. Each book in the series specialises in either language skills or aspects of the English language. It can be used either in class or by students working on their own.

Just Vocabulary consists of 24 units. Each unit is divided into two sections. In the first section, vocabulary for a variety of topic areas is introduced and practised. Topics include jobs and work, food and drink, and the weather.
The second section concentrates on functional areas such as telling the time, ordering food and asking for / giving directions.

All the dialogue and practice material has been recorded onto a CD, and there is an Audioscript at the back of the book.

Students will be able to use the book without needing explanations or guidance on the part of the teacher, and they can check their work in the comprehensive Answer Key at the back of the book. However, the units are also highly appropriate for work in class.

We hope you find this book a real asset and that you will also try the other books in the series: *Just Reading and Writing*, *Just Grammar* and *Just Listening and Speaking*.

A Vocabulary Useful phrases

1 Look at the pictures in Activity 2. Listen to Track 1. Number the phrases in the order you hear them.

Thank you! [1] That's OK. [ ] Excuse me. [ ]
Sorry! [ ] I don't understand. [ ] Sorry? [ ]
See you later! [ ] Bye! [ ]

2 Listen to Track 1 again. Write the phrases in the right place.

3 Listen to Track 1 again and repeat the phrases.

4 What do you say in these situations? Write a phrase.

Listen to Track 2 and check your answers.

Word Bank

Make a vocabulary notebook.

Make a 'Useful expressions' page. Write the expressions and a translation in your language.

Thank you. – Gracias.
That's OK. – De nada.

When you find new expressions add them to this page.

B Function Introducing someone

1 Listen to Track 3. Write the names of the people in the pictures.

Françoise Janie Mr Watanabe Ms Peters Steve

a .... b Steve c ....

d .... e ....

2 Listen to Track 3 again. Write the phrases in the table.

Hello Good morning I'm ... Nice to meet you
Hi This is ... Pleased to meet you

Greeting	Introducing	Responding
Hello		

3 Now complete the conversations with one of the phrases.

STEVE: Hello, (a) I'm Steve.

JANIE: (b) .... Steve. How are you?

(c) .... Janie.

STEVE: Janie, (d) .... Françoise.

JANIE: (e) ...., Françoise.

FRANÇOISE: (f) .... too.

MAN: Good morning, Ms Peters.

MS PETERS: (g) ....

MAN: (h) .... Mr Watanabe.

MS PETERS: (i) ...., Mr Watanabe.

MR WATANABE: (j) .... too, Ms Peters.

Listen to Track 3 again and check your answers.

UNIT 2

A Vocabulary Countries and nationalities

1 Write the names of the countries in *a–f* on the map below.

China	France	Korea	Mexico	Russia	South Africa

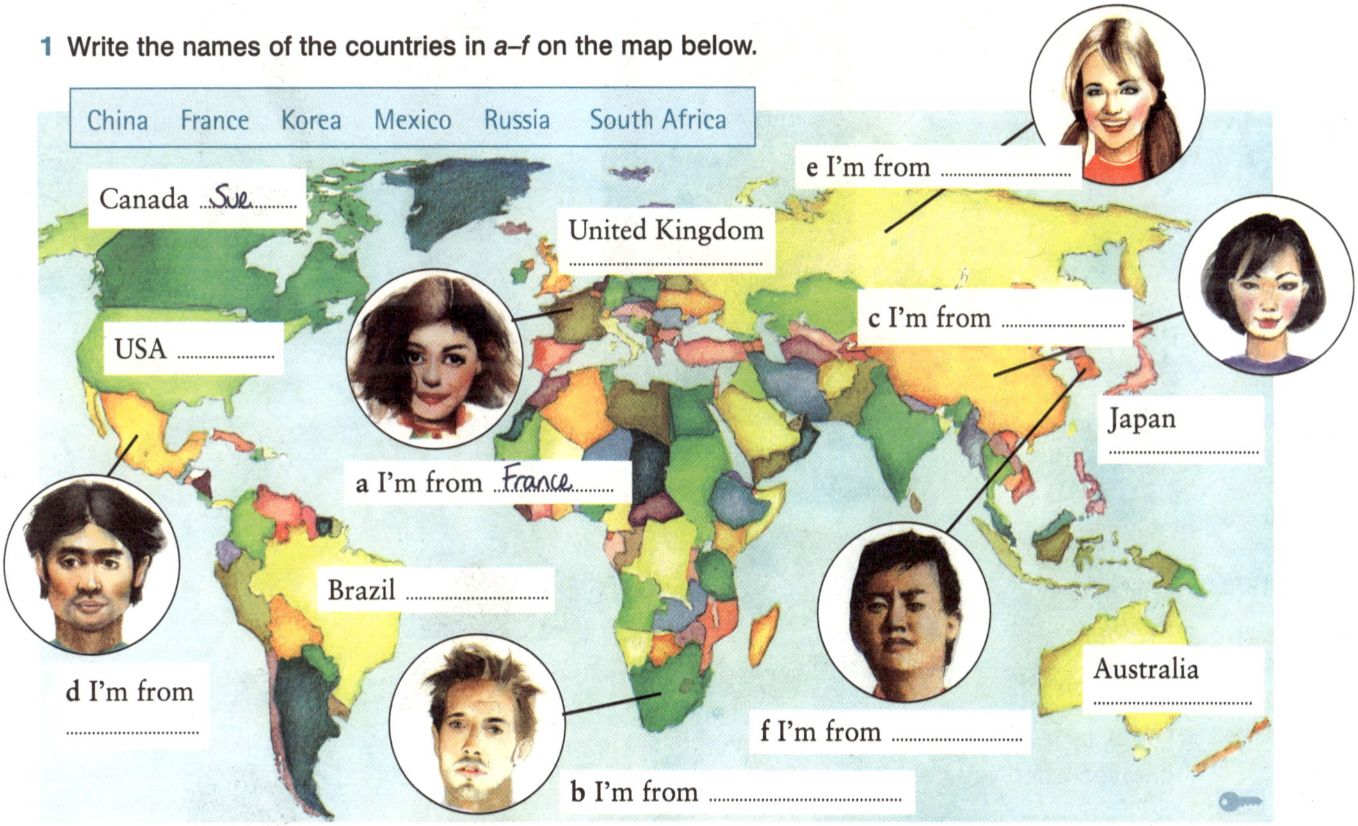

2 Listen to Track 4 and check your answers.

3 Listen to Track 5. Write the name of the person in the right place on the map in Activity 1.

Sue Milton Miranda Ken Karen Ed

4 Match the name of the country with the nationality.

a Japan	1 Brazilian
b the UK	2 Korean
c the USA	3 Russian
d France	4 American
e South Africa	5 Australian
f China	6 French
g Mexico	7 British
h Canada	8 Chinese
i Korea	9 Japanese
j Russia	10 Mexican
k Brazil	11 South African
l Australia	12 Canadian

5 Listen to Track 5 again and underline the stressed syllable in the six nationality words (in the list in Activity 4).

6 Practise saying the words in the same way.

Word Bank

Writing words that are related together helps you to remember them.

In your notebook, make a table with these related words.

Country	Nationality
France	French
Mexico	Mexican

B Function Greetings

1 Listen to Track 6 and match the three conversations to the pictures.

2 Listen to Track 6 again. Tick (✓) the phrases when you hear them.

Greeting	
Hi!	
Hello.	
Good morning.	
Good afternoon.	✓
Good evening.	
Question	
How are you?	
How's it going?	
Answer	
Fine, thanks.	
Very well, thank you.	
Fine, thank you.	
Very well, thanks.	
Not bad, thanks.	
And you?	
You?	

3 Write conversations in these situations.

a ....

....

....

b ....

....

....

c ....

....

....

d ....

....

....

Practise your conversations.

UNIT 3

A Vocabulary Jobs and occupations

1 Label pictures *a–l* with the name of the job or occupation.

accountant actor architect cleaner cook doctor engineer nurse singer student taxi driver teacher

a actor

b

c

d

e

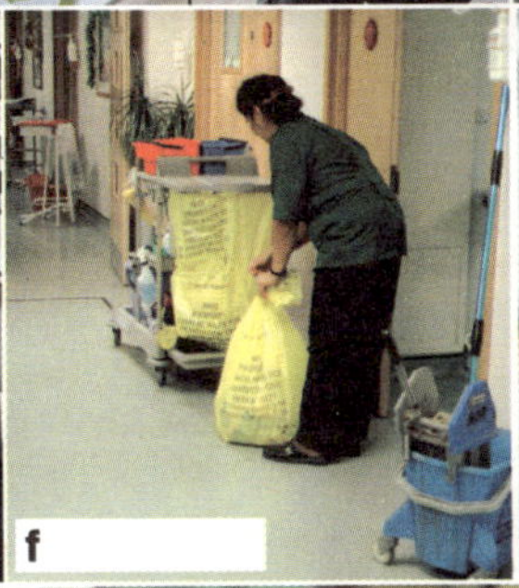
f

g

h

i

j

k

l

Listen to Track 7 and check your answers.

2 Match the occupations with the workplaces.

a office accountant
b kitchen ....
c school ....
d theatre ....
e hospital ....
f street ....

Common ending for occupations: *-er*

He *cleans* offices. → a *clean**er***
She *sings* in a band. → a *sing**er***
They *teach* children. → *teach**ers***

3 Write a sentence about the occupations in Activity 1.

a He works in a theatre. He is an actor.
b ....
c ....
d ....
e ....
f ....
g ....
h ....
i ....
j ....
k ....
l ....

Word Bank

Grouping words together helps you to remember them.

Copy this table into your notebook and complete it. Divide the occupations into ones that begin with a vowel sound and ones that begin with a consonant sound.

a	an
taxi driver	architect

B Function Talking about jobs

1 Listen to the conversations on Track 8 and write the names of the people under the picture.

Richard Marshall Linda Marie

....

....

....

....

2 Listen to Track 8 again. Complete the table with these phrases.

What do you do? I'm a(n) .... That's interesting.

Asking about jobs	Answering	Reacting
What's your job?	(b)	Oh, really?
(a)		That's great.
		(c) ....

UNIT 4

A Vocabulary Family members

1 **Look at the picture. Fill in the blanks in sentences *a–h* with words from the box. Clue: unscramble the words in brackets!**

Just note

Tom**'s** six. = Tom **is** six.

Tom**'s** father = Mike

Family members	
mother(s)	wife (wives)
father(s)	uncle(s)
son(s)	aunt(s)
daughter(s)	cousin(s)
brother(s)	grandchild
sister(s)	(grandchildren)
husband(s)	grandmother(s)

a Bob and Mike are ....brothers.... (thersbro).

b Kirsty and Pippa are .... (ssstier).

c Bob and Leyla are .... (ubahnsd) and .... (fewi).

d Tim and Pippa are .... (ouinscs).

e Keiko and Mike are Tim and Tom's .... (thermo) and .... (herfat).

f Bob and Leyla have four children: two .... (ossn) and two .... (dtersaugh).

g Lucia is a happy .... (gramotndher). She has seven .... (dcgreranihldn) – four grandsons and three granddaughters.

h The children have one .... (leunc) and one .... (ntau).

2 **Now listen to Track 9 and check your answers. Practise introducing the family.**

Example:

This is Bob. Bob has four children ...

Word Bank

Grouping words together helps you to remember them.

In your notebook, write words for family members in two columns, *Male* and *Female*.

Male	Female
grandfather	grandmother

B Function Talking about age

1 Listen to Track 10 and write the numbers as you listen. Practise saying the numbers.

one .....1.....	two	three	four	five	six	seven	eight	nine	ten ....
eleven	twelve	thirteen	fourteen	fifteen	sixteen	seventeen	eighteen	nineteen	twenty ....
thirty	forty	fifty	sixty	seventy	eighty	ninety	a hundred		

2 Write the numbers on the lines.

26 ....twenty-six.......... minutes
31 .... days
45 .... minutes
69 .... per cent
77 .... years old
83 .... per cent
89 .... years old
94 .... per cent

3 Listen to Track 11. Match the four conversations with pictures *a–d*.

a ....

b .....1.....

c ....

d ....

4 Listen to Track 11 again. Tick (✓) the sentences when you hear them.

Asking about age	Answering
a How old are you?	**1** Three months old.
b How old is she?	**2** I'm 55.
c How old is it? ✓	**3** She's 100 years old today.

Now match the questions with the answers.

5 Work out the ages. Complete the sentences.

Lucy 2006

Your house?

Saturday

You?

Daniel 1958

a .....How..... old .... Lucy?
.... old.

b How old is your house?
It's .... years old.

c .... old .... the dogs?
Only ....

d .... you?
I ....

e How .... is Daniel?
He' ....

A Vocabulary Everyday actions

1 Label the pictures with words from the box.

get up   go to bed   go to work   have a shower   have breakfast
read the paper   relax   sleep   watch television   work

2 Listen to Track 12 and check your answers.

Word Bank

Writing verbs and nouns as phrases helps you to remember which words go together.

Write the new words in groups with the correct verb in your notebook.

go	to bed
	to work
have	a shower

3 Make ten true sentences.

Example: I don't work in an office every day.

I	(don't)	go have read watch work	in an office to work breakfast a book a shower in a shop to bed television the paper DVDs	(on Sundays). (every day).

4 Practise saying your sentences.

B Function Telling the time

1 **Listen to Track 13. Match the four situations with pictures *a–d*.**

2 **Listen to Track 13 again. Complete the information in the table.**

Asking the time
Do you have the time, please? (a) .... ? What's the time?
Asking the time of something
(b) .... ?
Telling the time
It's (c) .... o'clock. It's quarter to twelve. It's half past twelve. It's twenty-five past twelve. It's (d) .... minutes past twelve.
Giving the time of something
At (e) ....

When do we say *o'clock*? When do we say *minutes*?

3 **Put the words in the correct order to make questions.**

a It's 12 o'clock midday in London. What / is / time / it / in San Francisco / ? ....
What time is it in San Francisco?

b It's 3.15 p.m. in London. What / the / 's / time / in Mexico City / ? ....

c It's 4.45 a.m. in Buenos Aires. in / Paris / time / it / is / What / ? ....

d It's 6.30 p.m. in Beijing, China. time / in Sydney / ? / is / What / it ....

e It's 9.03 a.m. in New York. the / time / in São Paulo / What / 's / ? ....

f It's 7.20 p.m. in London. in your country / time / What / it / is / ? ....

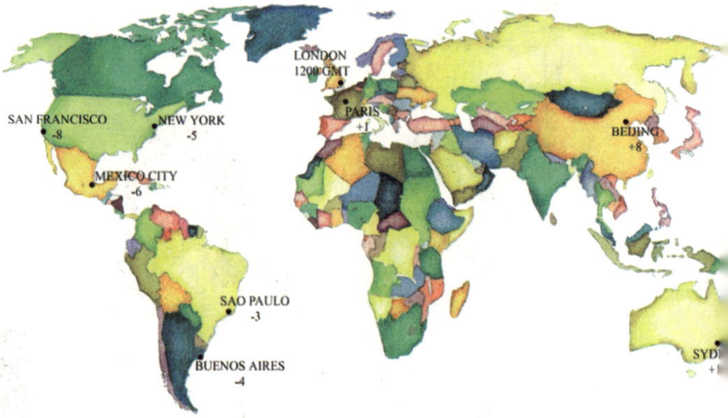

4 **Look at the map. Work out the times and answer the questions in Activity 3.**

Example: It's 12 o'clock midday in London.
What time is it in San Francisco?

a It's four o'clock in the morning.

b ....

c ....

d ....

e ....

f ....

5 **Listen to Track 14 and speak after the beep.**

UNIT 6

A Vocabulary Food and drink

1 Look at the pictures. Copy and complete the table with your favourite foods.

Drinks	tea
Snacks	crisps
Breakfast foods	bread
Lunch foods	cheese
Dinner foods	meat

2 Listen to Track 15. Fill in the blanks with the words you hear.

A: What .... you like to have for breakfast?

B: I .... bread and coffee. .... you?

Word Bank

Grouping words together as in Activity 1 helps you to remember them.

In your notebook, make two lists:
– food you normally eat cold
– food you normally eat hot.

3 Cross out the word that is different.

a tea coffee juice ~~cake~~
b cheese milk chicken ice cream
c cake soda sandwich bread
d vegetables salad fruit crisps
e chocolate crisps eggs sweets
f fish chocolate sweets cake

4 Chat with Stella. Answer her questions.

STELLA: It's one o'clock – lunchtime! In Britain, we have a small meal at lunch and a big meal in the evening. What about your country?

YOU: (a) ....

STELLA: I like to have tea, milk and bread for breakfast. And you?

YOU: (b) ....

STELLA: What about lunch? I like a sandwich and some fruit.

YOU: (c) ....

STELLA: Dinner is at 7.00. We have meat or fish and vegetables. What about you?

YOU: (d) ....

STELLA: I like snacks in the afternoon, chocolate for example. How about you?

YOU: (e) ....

STELLA: Back to work now. Talk to you soon!

Listen to Track 16. Talk to Stella and speak after the beep.

B Function Ordering food

1 Listen to two dialogues in a cafeteria on Track 17. Complete the dialogues.

1

GIRL: Next please.

MAN: A ...cheese sandwich... and .... chocolate cake, please.

GIRL: Coming up. And to drink?

MAN: Sorry?

GIRL: What would you like to drink?

MAN: I'll have a .... Milk, no sugar.

GIRL: Sure. That's .... , please.

2

MAN: Can I help you?

WOMAN: I'd like .... and a ....

MAN: Sure. Anything else?

WOMAN: Can I have some ketchup, please?

MAN: Here you are. That's .... , please.

WOMAN: Thanks.

2 Complete the table with words from Track 17.

Taking the order	Ordering	Saying the price
And to drink?	A cheese sandwich, please.	That's £6.25, please.
(a) .... ?	(d)	
(b) .... ?	(e)	
(c) .... ?	(f) .... ?	

Practise saying the dialogues.

3 Look at the waiter's notes. Order the food.

WAITER: Can I help you?

YOU: (a) ....

....

WAITER: What would you like to drink?

YOU: (b) ....

WAITER: Anything else?

YOU: (c) ....

WAITER: That's £5.20, please.

Listen to Track 18 and check your answers.

Table 3 Waiter: Bob

Cheese sandwich, chocolate ice cream, coffee (milk, no sugar)

4 Now you are the waiter. Ask the questions in Activity 3. Listen to Track 19 and speak after the beep. Write the person's order.

Table 4 Waiter: ....

A Vocabulary Hobbies

1 **Complete the sentences with the name of the person or people or with the name of the hobby.**

doing puzzles
going shopping
going to the cinema
listening to music
playing sports
playing video games
reading
travelling
watching TV
working out

a Sasha likes *travelling* .
b .... likes doing puzzles.
c Jake and Sandra like ....
d .... likes playing video games.
e Johanna likes ....
f .... likes working out.
g Mark and Patrick like ....
h .... like playing sports.
i Karl likes ....
j .... like going shopping.

Listen to Track 20 and check your answers.

2 **Sports: *play* or *go*?**

football	basketball	volleyball	running	tennis
baseball	swimming	skiing	skateboarding	golf

I like playing ...	I like going ...
football	*running*

3 **Look at the table and write sentences about the people.**

Jane ♥	Marie ♥	Kevin and Trudy ♥

a *Jane likes playing football.*
b ....
c ....
d ....
e ....
f ....

B Function Agreeing and disagreeing on statements

1 Listen to the conversations *a–e* on Track 21. Do the speakers agree (A) or disagree (D)?

a ...D... b .... c .... d .... e ....

2 Complete this table with the language you hear.

I agree. That's not right. I don't think so.
Of course. Certainly not.

Agreeing	Disagreeing
I think so.	(c) ....
(a)	I don't agree.
That's right.	(d) ....
(b)	Of course not.
Certainly.	(e) ....

3 Match the questions and the answers.

1 We love playing football. It's fun. [b]
2 Ronaldinho is Mexican, right? [ ]
3 You like going shopping, don't you? [ ]
4 Susie really likes doing puzzles. [ ]

a Certainly not. He's Brazilian.
b I agree. It's great fun.
c No, that's not right. She likes reading.
d Of course I do.

Listen to Track 22 and check your answers.

4 Agree or disagree with these statements.

a You like travelling, don't you?

....

b English is fun.

....

c Shakira is French, right?

....

d I like Chinese food. It's delicious.

....

e You like Italian food, right?

....

f Angelina Jolie is German, isn't she?

....

g Watching TV is boring.

....

Now listen to Track 23 and speak after the beep.

UNIT 8

A Vocabulary Parts of the body

1 Label the picture with one of the words from the box.

arm back chest ear eye foot
hand head leg mouth nose
stomach throat tooth

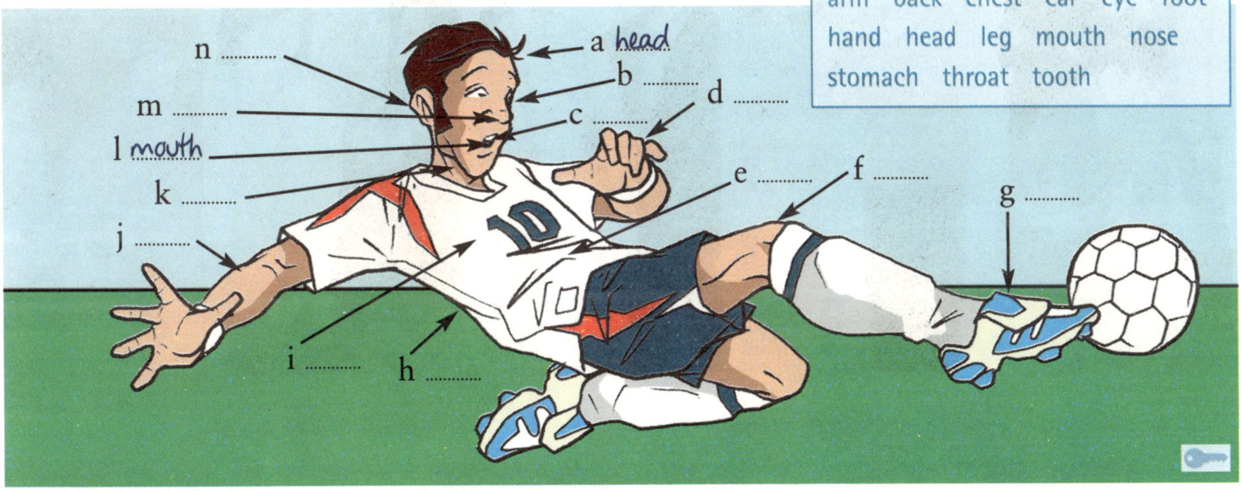

2 Complete these sentences with one of the words in Activity 1.

a You use your ......head...... to think.
b You use your .... and .... to walk.
c You need your .... to sing.
d You usually lie down on your ....
e Food goes into your ....
f You use your .... to smell.
g You see and hear things with your .... and ....
h You eat food with your .... and your ....
i You use your .... to breathe.
j You use your .... and .... to drive a car.

Listen to Track 24 and check your answers.

Just note
Singular: tooth foot
Plural: teeth feet

Word Bank
Using pictures can help you to remember vocabulary.
Draw a picture of a person in your notebook and label all the parts of the body.

3 Complete this table with all the parts of the body that you need to do these things.

eat	play football	use a computer	work out	listen to an MP3 player
mouth				

B Function Asking and talking about health

1 Listen to five people's problems on Track 25. Match the five conversations with pictures *a–e*.

a ....

b ....

c ....

d ....

e .....1.....

2 Listen to Track 25 again and write the number of the conversation in the boxes.

Asking		Answering		Reacting	
a How do you feel?		**f** Her back hurts.		**k** Oh, I'm sorry to hear that.	1
b What's wrong with Sarah?		**g** I have a problem.	1	**l** Oh dear.	
c What's the matter?	1	**h** I feel awful. My throat hurts and my head hurts.		**m** Poor James.	
d What's wrong?		**i** His stomach hurts.		**n** Oh, you poor thing.	
e What's the matter with James?		**j** I've got a cold.		**o** Oh dear. I'm sorry to hear that.	

3 Find three conversations here. Write them in the correct order.

He's got a problem. [ ]
I feel awful. My head hurts. [ ]
Poor Janie. [ ]
What's wrong with Billy? [ ]
Her throat hurts. [ ]
You poor thing! [ ]
How do you feel? [ ]
Oh, dear. Poor Billy. [ ]
What's the matter with Janie? [1]

a What's the matter with Janie?

b ....

c ....

Now listen to Track 26 and check your answers.

4 Listen to Track 27 and speak after the beep.

UNIT 9

A Vocabulary Clothes

dress jacket shirt shoes skirt socks
suit sweater tie trousers T-shirt

1 Match the words with the items of clothing.

Now listen to Track 28 and check your answers.

2 Add other clothes words you know to the diagram.

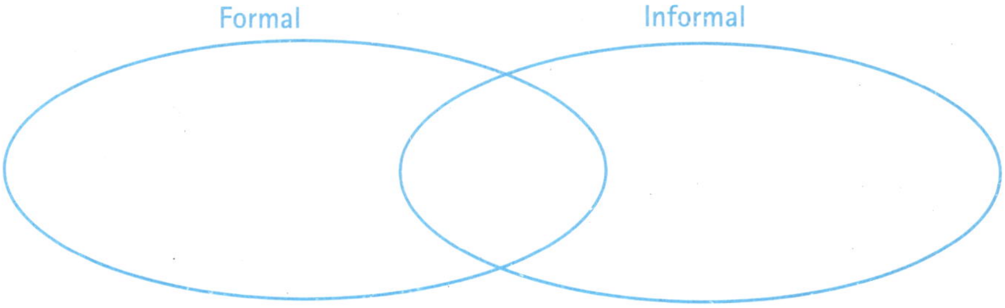

3 Write the words in the correct column.

a	a pair of
dress	shoes

4 Complete these sentences with names of clothes.

a How much is that pair of s*hoes*?

b I need to buy a new s___ and t__ for a wedding.

c Do you like these t_______?

d I need a d____ for a party.

e Laura wears a s____ to work.

f John wears a s____ and j_____ to work.

g On Fridays we wear T-s_____ in the office.

Word Bank

Grouping words together helps you to remember them.

Copy the diagram into your notebook. Write all the clothes words you know in the diagram.

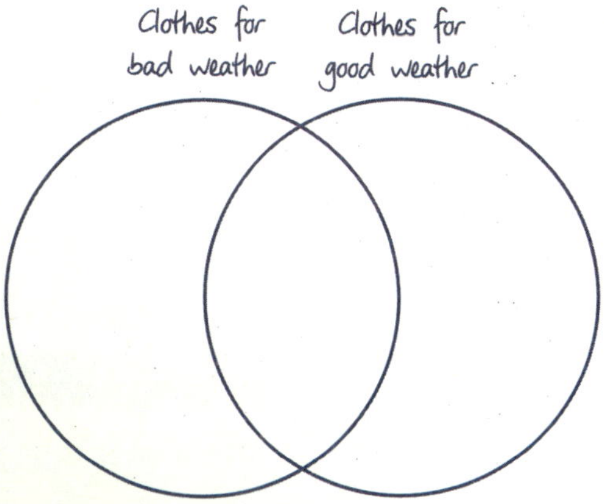

B Function Buying things

1 Listen to two conversations in shops on Track 29 and circle the words you hear.

a CUSTOMER: Excuse me. How much is that (1) *skirt / shirt*?
ASSISTANT: It's £25.
CUSTOMER: Do you have a (2) *small / medium / large*?
ASSISTANT: Yes. Do you want to (3) *try / buy* it?
CUSTOMER: Yes, please.

b CUSTOMER: I'd like a (4) *tie / suit*.
ASSISTANT: Yes, of course. What about (5) *this / that* one?
CUSTOMER: How much (6) *does it / do they* cost?
ASSISTANT: £10.
CUSTOMER: Thanks. I'll take (7) *this one / that one / it*.
ASSISTANT: Here you are. That's £10.
CUSTOMER: Thank you.

2 Complete the tables.

BUYING THINGS 1

Asking for something
I'd (a) .... a shirt.
Do you have a small / (b) .... / large?
Asking about price
How (c)........... is that shirt?
How much is it?
How much (d) .... it cost?
How much are those shoes?
How much do they (e) ....?

BUYING THINGS 2

Assistant
It's £250.
What (f) .... this one?
Do you (g) .... to try it?
Do you want to buy it?
Customer
I'll (h) .... this one.
I'll take it.

3 Who says this? The customer or the assistant?

a It's £1.50 a loaf.
b £50. Do you want to try it?
c I'll take two, please. How much is that?
d I'd like a dress.
e Excuse me. How much is this bread?
f Certainly. What about this black one?
g No, thank you.
h How much does it cost?
i That's £3.00. Anything else?
j Yes, please.

Customer
c, ...

Assistant
a, ...

4 Make two conversations.

1 Customer: Excuse me. How much is this bread?
....

2 ....
....
....

Now listen to Track 30 and speak after the beep.

5 Listen to Track 31 and check your answers.

UNIT 10

A Vocabulary Actions

1 Look at these words. Check the meaning and complete the table.

always never occasionally often sometimes usually

More frequent ⟶ Less frequent

100%	80%	60–80%	40–50%	10–20%	0%
always					never

2 Look at the actions. Which of the actions do you do? When do you do them? Write sentences.

Example: I sometimes ride a bicycle to work. I often drive a car. I never jump or climb.

3 Match the verbs with the nouns.

a throw	horse
b hit	tree
c ride	bicycle
d drive	car
e climb	ball (a)
	motorbike
	mountain

4 Complete these questions with an action verb.

a Do you ...drive... a car to work or to school?
b Do you ever .... a bicycle in the city?
c Do you ever .... a motorbike?
d Do you ever .... trees?
e Do you .... at parties?

5 Now listen to questions *a–j* on Track 32 and speak after the beep.

B Function Asking for language help

1 Listen to Track 33. How many times does Daniela ask for help – once, twice, three times or four times?

2 Listen to Track 33 again. Complete Daniela's lines with language from the table.

Asking for language help	
Help with difficult words:	How do you say (small money)? What does (welfare) mean?
Help with difficult sentences:	I don't understand. Can you speak slowly, please? Can you say that again, please?

a Sorry? I don't understand. Can you speak ... ?

b Sorry. What .... ?

c .... please?

d Oh! I'm sorry, I haven't got ... how .... 'small money'?

3 Match the questions with the answers.

a what does 'clothes' mean? [3]

b how do you say 'not very often'? [ ]

c what does 'magazine' mean? [ ]

d How do you say 'the part of your body where food goes'? [ ]

1 Occasionally

2 Stomach

3 Things we wear

4 It's something to read and it has a lot of pictures.

Now listen to Track 34 and check your answers.

4 Put the words in order to make a conversation.

a want / you / to / come / Do / cinema / us / the / with / to / ?

Do you want to come to the cinema with us?

b speak / please / Can / slowly, / you / ? / more

....

c great / this / There's / movie / evening / a / .

....

d 'movie' / mean / does / What / ?

....

e film / a / It's / . ...

f that / say / you / Can / please / again, / ?

....

g cinema / is / movie / A / the / at / a / film / .

....

h love / movie / go / I'd / the / to / to / !

....

Now listen to Track 35 and check your answers.

5 Now listen to Track 36 and speak after the beep.

A Vocabulary Hair, body and face

1 Look at the pictures. Write the words in the correct place in *a–f*.

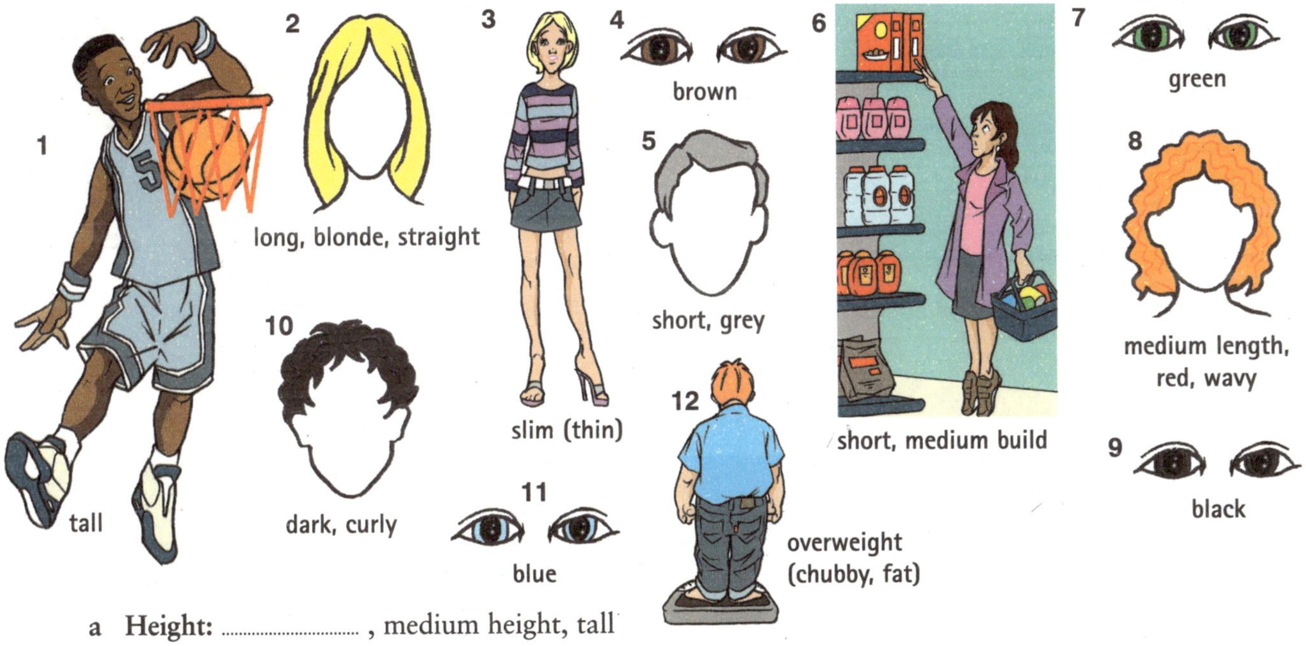

a Height: .... , medium height, tall

b Weight: ....thin.... , ... , ... , ... , ... , fat

c Hair – length: short, ... , ...

d Hair – colour: .... , ... , ... , ...

e Hair – type: .... , ... , ...

f Eyes: .... , ... , ... , ...

2 Bingo Choose eight words or phrases from Activity 1. Write them down. Listen to Track 37. Tick the words when you hear them. If you hear them all, say 'Bingo!'.

Word Bank

Personalising words helps you to remember them.

Copy the table into your notebook and complete it with details of friends and family.

	Height	Weight	Hair	Eyes
mother	tall	slim	black	blue
brother				
best friend				

Just note

It is not polite to say to people that they are *thin*, *chubby* or *fat*.

3 Read these sentences and write the name of the person.

a He is short and a bit chubby. He's got long blonde hair and blue eyes. ....

b She is tall and she is a bit overweight. She has long dark hair and dark eyes. ....

Now listen to Track 38 and check your answers.

4 Write sentences about the other two people.

....

....

....

....

....

....

Listen to Track 39 and speak after the beep.

B Function Describing people

1 Listen to Track 40, a conversation in a model agency, and look at the cards below. Which model do the people choose, Claudia, Sky or Simone?

Claudia Bianchi
Age: 21
Height: 1.72 m
Weight: 60 kg

Sky Roberts
Age: 21
Height: 1.72 m
Weight: 58 kg

Simone Johnson
Age: 21
Height: 1.75 m
Weight: 63 kg

2 Complete the dialogue with questions from the table.

Describing people

Asking about age: How old (is he/she)?
Asking about height: How tall (is he/she)?
Asking about weight: How much (does he/she) weigh?
Asking about appearance: What (does he/she) look like?

WOMAN: I have the perfect model for the fashion show.
MAN: (a) How old ... ?
WOMAN: Twenty-one.
MAN: (b) .... ?
WOMAN: She's got green eyes, long dark hair, very straight. Lovely dark skin.
MAN: (c) .... ?
WOMAN: One metre seventy-five.
MAN: (d) .... ?
WOMAN: Sixty-three kilos. She's very slim.
MAN: Yes, I agree with you. She's perfect for the job.

Just note

British English		American English
he/she has got	=	he/she has

Listen to Track 40 again and check your answers.

3 The five statements/questions in *1–5* should be followed by a question *a–e*. Put them in the correct order.

1 Do you know Joe? [e]
2 He's got short blonde hair and blue eyes. [ ]
3 About 1.85, I think. [ ]
4 I don't know. He's slim, maybe about 90 kilos. [ ]
5 About 25. [ ]

a I think I know him. How old is he?
b Is he thin? How much does he weigh?
c Oh, yes, I know him. What about him?
d Hmm. How tall is he?
e I'm not sure. What does he look like?

Listen to Track 41 and check your answers.

Just note
5′5″ = five foot five (1.65 m)
125 LBS = 125 pounds (57 kg)

4 Complete this conversation about Maxine.

DRIVING LICENCE
D01234567

MAXINE SANDERS
AGE: 21
HEIGHT: 5′5″
WEIGHT: 125 LBS
EYES: BROWN
HAIR: BLACK

YOU: (a) Do you know Maxine?
MAN: I'm not sure. What does she look like?
YOU: (b) ....
MAN: Hmm. How tall is she?
YOU: (c) ....
MAN: How much does she weigh?
YOU: (d) ....
MAN: Yes, I think I know her. How old is she?
YOU: (e) ....

Now listen to Track 42 and speak after the beep.

UNIT 12

A Vocabulary Interacting

Just note

every	day
once a	week
twice a	month
three times a	year

1 How often do you do these things? Write sentences about you.

Example: I send emails five times a day.

send emails

send text messages

go on the Internet

send a fax

take (and send) photos

leave a (voice) message

play games

make a phone call

Now listen to Track 43 and speak after the beep.

2 Match the words in the columns to make sentences.

Sherry talks Tom likes playing games Leave Mike a message Find the information Call me	on	his answering machine. the Internet. the phone for hours! my mobile phone. the computer.
Jane always sends her reports I often send photos We sometimes order food	by	phone. fax. email.

Example: Sherry talks on the phone for hours!

Listen to Track 44 and check your answers.

3 Look at the machines in Activity 2. Which do you use to do the actions in Activity 1? Write sentences.

I leave voice messages on an answering machine.

....

Word Bank

Remember to write the new words in groups with the correct verb.

Write the phrases in your notebook.

send	emails
	text messages
	a fax
talk	on the phone

4 **Complete these sentences with a verb. Some words may be used more than once.**

send go take leave play make

a I often ...leave... messages on Jane's answering machine.

b Do you want to .... a video game on the computer?

c I need to .... a call on my mobile phone.

d Why don't you .... a text message?

e You can find his address if you .... online.

f I'm going to .... photographs with my new digital camera.

g She has a fax machine, so you can .... her a fax.

5 **Describe what people are doing in this picture.**

Ron is making a phone call.

....

....

....

....

B Function Using the telephone

1 **Listen to two telephone conversations on Track 45. Answer the questions.**

a How many people call Jodi?
b Does Jodi speak to Robin? Why or why not?
c Does Jodi speak to her manager? Why or why not?

2 **Put the sentences in the correct place in the conversations.**

Hello? This is Robin. Who's speaking?
Do you want to leave a message?
Can I take a message?

1	2
BOY: Hello?	BOY: Hello?
ROBIN: **(a)**	MANAGER: Can I speak to Jodi Parker, please?
Can I speak to Jodi, please?	BOY: She's at the cinema. **(c)** ....
BOY: Sure. Hold on …	MANAGER: It's her manager.
Sorry, Robin. Jodi says she is not here.	BOY: Oh. Then Jodi's in bed with a cold.
(b)	**(d)** ....

Listen to Track 45 again and check your answers.

3 Complete this dialogue.

MARIANA: Hello?

FERNANDO: (a) ......Hello.......

MARIANA: Can I (b) .... Lyndsay, please?

FERNANDO: She's not here. (c) .... ?

MARIANA: (d) .... Mariana.

FERNANDO: Do you want to (e) .... ?

MARIANA: Yes, please. Can you tell her that Mariana and Robin aren't coming to the party, because Robin is sick.

FERNANDO: Sure, I'll tell her.

MARIANA: (f) ....

FERNANDO: (g) ....

Listen to Track 46 and check your answers.

4 Now listen to Track 47

Speak after the beep.

5 Complete this form about the message.

MESSAGES

Message for:

____

Message taken by:

____

Message:

____

____

____

Returned your call ☐

Please call ☐

Will call you ☐

UNIT 13

A Vocabulary Rooms and furniture

1 Find these words in this word search.

S	O	F	A	C	B	E	G	D	I	R	F
T	S	G	H	I	O	K	J	E	F	E	R
O	W	Y	I	U	N	H	Y	S	Q	W	K
V	D	T	Z	X	P	B	N	K	M	O	E
E	W	A	Y	G	I	P	M	F	V	H	C
D	B	B	C	U	R	T	A	I	N	S	M
Q	R	L	I	R	P	L	D	L	A	M	P
H	J	E	K	M	N	B	R	S	E	T	U
K	O	P	L	T	E	L	I	O	T	E	P
S	Y	B	E	D	W	B	A	M	N	K	B
X	P	A	H	M	L	U	H	Y	T	R	S
R	E	T	U	P	M	O	C	I	V	Q	D

TV bed sofa chair curtains
rug desk stove shower toilet
lamp computer table fridge

2 Now write the words from Activity 1 on these pictures.

a TV

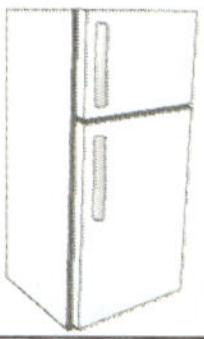
b ....

c ....

d ....

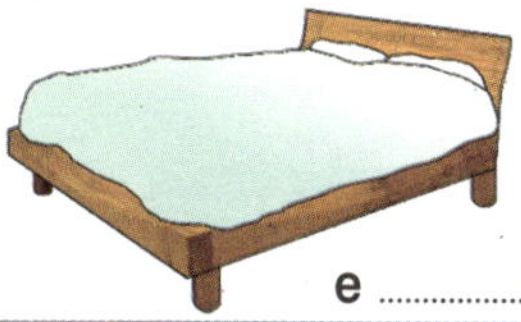
e ....

f ....

g ....

h ....

i ....

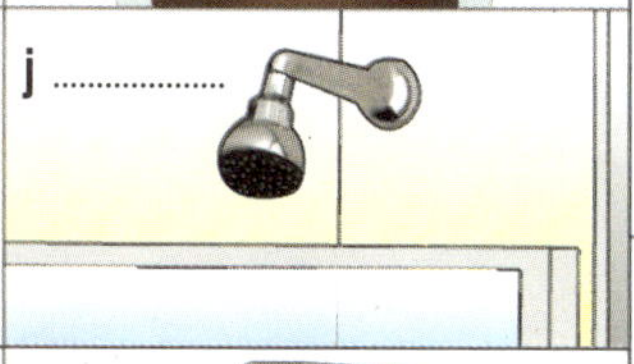
j ....

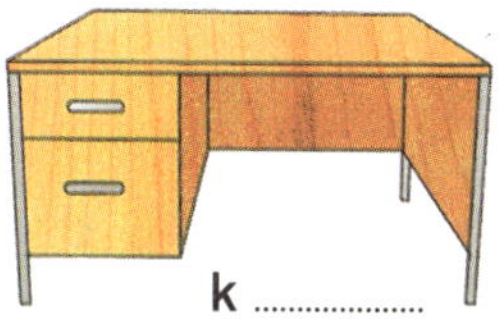
k ....

l ....

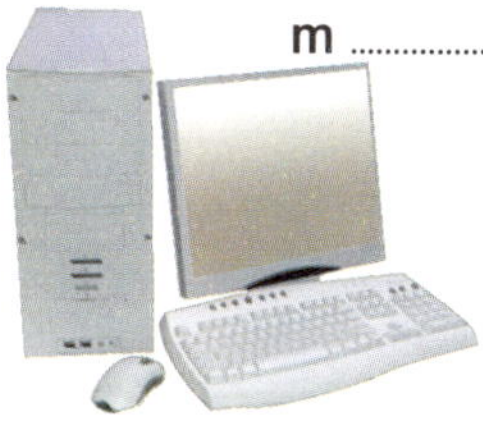
m ....

n ....

3 Where do the things from Activity 2 go in this house? Write the words on the plan.

Now listen to Track 48 and check your answers.

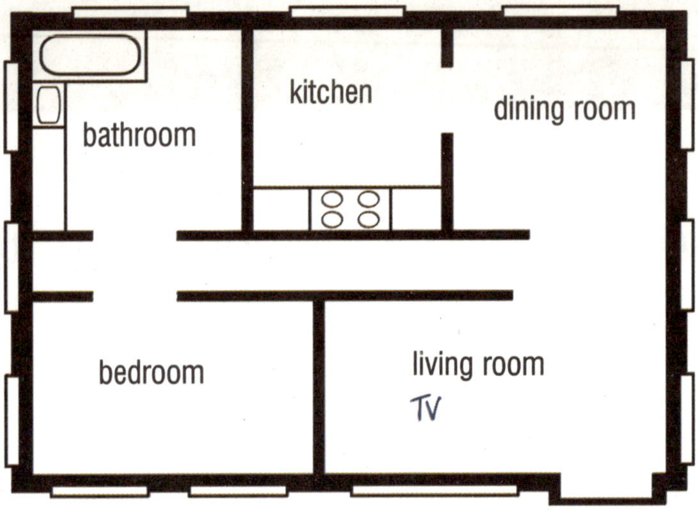

Word Bank

Personalising words helps you to remember them.

Draw a plan of your house or flat in your notebook and write the words for furniture in the correct room.

B Function Looking for something

1 Where is it? Listen to Track 49. Four people are looking for something. Choose the correct picture.

Example: *a–2*

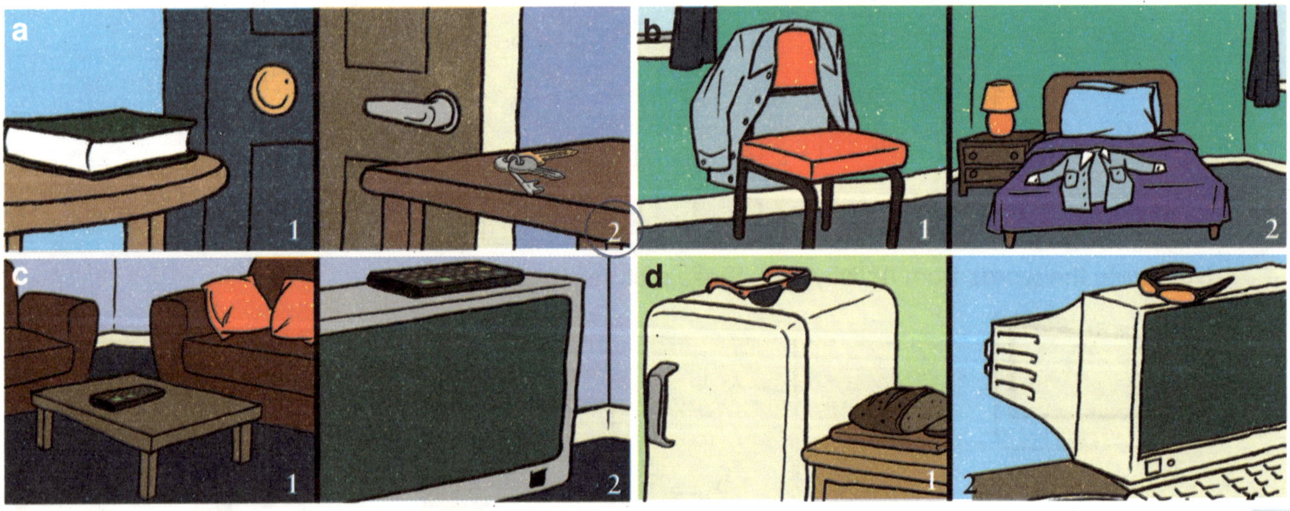

2 Listen to Track 49 again and complete the table with the words you hear.

Asking	Answering	Finding
(a) ....?	(b)	(d) ....
Where's ... ?	(c) .... ?	(e) ....
	Are they ... ?	(f) .... they are.
		There it is.
		Here they are.

3 Find two conversations here.

Oh, yes. Here it is. [ ]
In the living room. [ ]
Where's the newspaper? [ ]
Are they in the living room? [ ]
Where are my glasses? [ ]
No, it isn't under the newspaper. [ ]
Have you seen my watch? [1]
Oh, yes, here they are, next to the TV. [ ]
Are they on the fridge? [ ]
Is it in the bathroom? [ ]
No, they aren't in the kitchen. [ ]
No. Is it under the newspaper? [ ]

Conversation 1

MAN: Have you seen my watch?
WOMAN: ....
....
....
....
....
....

Conversation 2

WOMAN: ....
MAN: ....
....
....
....
....
....
....

Listen to Track 50 and check your answers.

4 Write a conversation in this situation.

KENNY: Have you seen my keys?

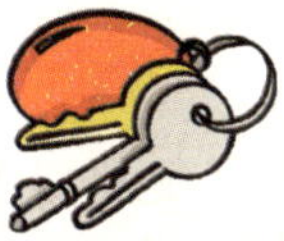

MARIE: No. (a) ....?

KENNY: No, they aren't.

MARIE: (b) ....?

KENNY: No.

MARIE: (c) ....?

KENNY: Oh, yes. Here they are. Thanks.

Listen to Track 51* and speak after the beep.

*Tracks 51–97 are on CD 2.

UNIT 14

A Vocabulary Public places

1 Look at these places and match them with the actions *a–n*.

1 shopping centre

2 hospital

3 bank

4 school

5 swimming pool

6 park

7 library

8 post office

9 sports centre

10 car park

11 supermarket

12 town hall

13 gym

14 cinema

a buy a stamp	[8]	f go to a meeting	[ ]	k buy some eggs	[ ]
b change some money	[ ]	g go swimming	[ ]	l take a maths test	[ ]
c borrow a book	[ ]	h buy some shoes	[ ]	m lose weight	[ ]
d go for a walk	[ ]	i see a doctor	[ ]	n see a film	[ ]
e park the car	[ ]	j play squash	[ ]		

Now listen to Track 52 and check your answers.

2 Do this crossword puzzle.

Across

2 Buy your groceries here
4 See a movie here
7 If your stomach hurts, go here
8 Borrow a book to read here
10 Get a stamp here

Down

1 Go for a walk here
2 Go swimming here
3 Go to meetings here
5 Get some money here
6 Work out here
9 Children learn here

Word Bank

Writing a definition of a word helps you to remember it.

In your notebook, write the names of the public places and what you can do there.

swimming pool – go swimming
post office – buy a stamp

B Function Asking for and giving directions

1 Listen to Track 53. Three people are asking for directions. Mark the places on the map.

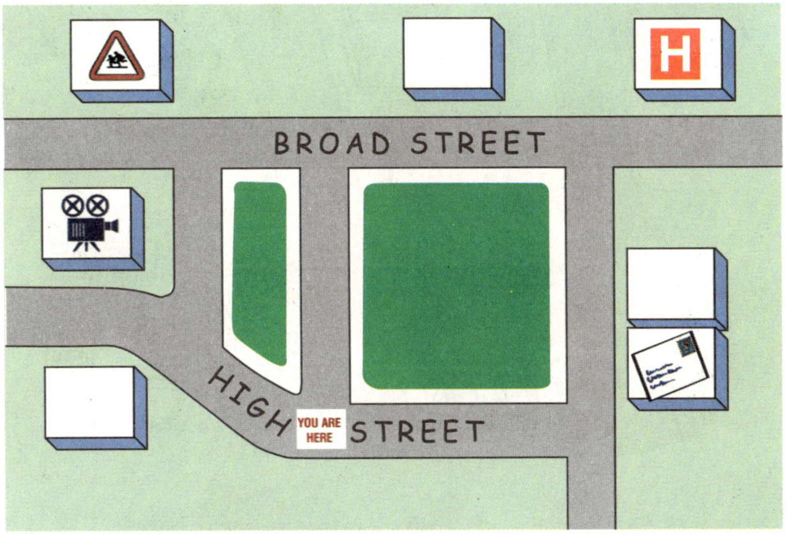

2 Complete this table with these words.

the left right is there
the right left

Asking for directions	Giving directions		
Where's the … ? (a) .... a(n) … near here?	Go	(straight) along up down	this street.
	Turn (b) .... ↱		
	It's on (c) .... >>		
	It's on (d) .... <<		
	Turn (e) .... ↰		

3 **Look at page 35 again. Complete these dialogues about places on the map with words from the table.**

a MAN: Excuse me, ... the cinema?

WOMAN: Go .... High Street and the cinema is ....

b WOMAN: Excuse me, ... a post office near here?

MAN: Yes. Go .... this street and .... left.

The post office is ....

c MAN: Excuse me, ... the hospital?

WOMAN: Go .... this street and .... right.

.... along Broad Street and the .... is on ....

d MAN: Excuse me, ... a school .... ?

WOMAN: .... up this street and .... left.

The school is ....

Listen to Track 54 and check your answers.

4 **Look at the map and complete the conversation.**

MAN: Excuse me, ...is there... a hospital near here?

WOMAN: Yes, dear. .... this street. Turn .... onto Green Street and .... the street.

The hospital is ....

Listen to Track 55 and check your answers.

5 **Write directions for these places.**

a Excuse me. Where's the library?

Go along Park Street. The library is on your right.

b Excuse me. Is there a supermarket near here?

....

c Excuse me. Where's the cinema? ....

d Excuse me. Where's the town hall? ....

6 **Now listen to Track 56 and speak after the beep.**

A Vocabulary Music

a clarinet

b trumpet

c drums

d violin

e piano

f saxophone

g guitar

1 Listen to Track 57 and match the name of the instrument with the music you hear.

Example: 1 e – piano

Which instruments do you like and which don't you like?

2 Match the musician with the type of music.

Mozart

Coldplay

Louis Armstrong

Eminem

Johnny Cash

Anastacia

jazz	classical	pop
country	dance	hip-hop

Example: Mozart – classical

3 Now write more examples under each type of music.

jazz: ....

classical: ....

pop: ....

country: ....

dance: ....

hip-hop: ....

4 Complete these ads with the names of musical instruments and types of music.

a
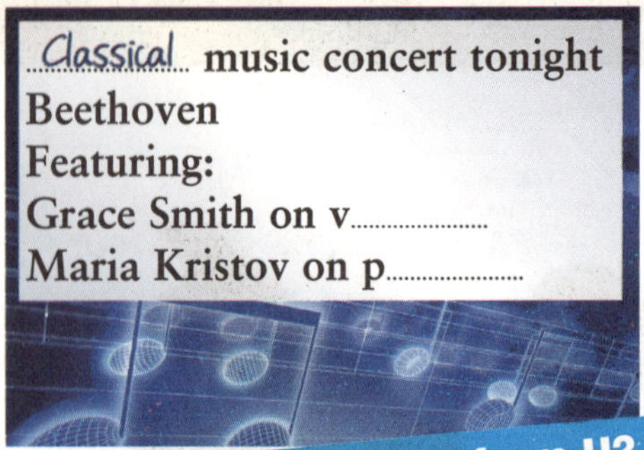

b

c

d

Word Bank

Grouping words together helps you to remember them.

Copy this table into your notebook and complete it.

Types of music	jazz				
Typical instruments used					

B Function Asking for and giving permission

1 Listen to Track 58 and match the four dialogues with the pictures.

2 Listen to Track 58 again. Complete the dialogues with these words.

Which one is most informal?

Asking for permission

1 BOY: .... leave the room?
TEACHER: Of course. But be quick.

2 BOY: Hey Mum, ... turn the TV on?
MOTHER: Not now. We're having dinner.

3 MAN: Mr Lacey, ... have the day off tomorrow?
MR LACEY: Hmm. We're not busy. Sure.

4 WOMAN 1: Excuse me. .... turn the music up?
WOMAN 2: Of course not.
WOMAN 1: Thank you.

May I | Can I | Do you mind if I

3 Now ask for permission and answer in these situations.

a

The boy wants to go into the classroom.

b

The girl wants to play the drums.

c

The girl wants to go out with her friends.

d

The man wants to open the window.

Listen to Track 59 and check your answers.

4 Put the words in the right order to make questions.

a turn / down / May / the / I / music / ?
May I turn the music down?

b window / mind / you / open / Do / I / the / if / ? ....

c go / I / party / Can / tonight / Joe's / to / ?
....

d the / mind / Do / watch / TV / you / I / if / ?
....

e car / borrow / your / I / Can / ?
....

f your / listen / Can / to / CDs / I / ?
....

5 Now match questions *a–f* with the answers.

1 No, I don't. Go ahead. [b]
2 Sure. Find something you like. [ ]
3 OK, but I need it this afternoon. [ ]
4 Yes, of course. It's very loud. [ ]
5 That's fine. See if there's a good programme. [ ]
6 No, you can't. You have school tomorrow. [ ]

Listen to Track 60 and check your answers.

6 Now listen to Track 61 and speak after the beep.

UNIT 16

A Vocabulary Studying

1 Name the subject.

art biology chemistry English geography history mathematics (maths) physics physical education (PE)

a ....art........

b ....

c ....

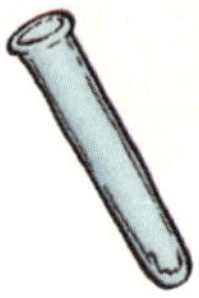

d ....

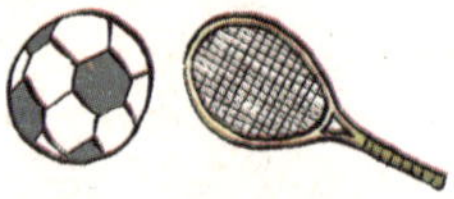

e ....

f ....

g ....

$E=MC^2$

h ....

$3x2+y=28$

i ....

2 Listen to Track 62 and write the subject in the diagram according to Martha's opinion.

	easy	difficult
interesting	history	
boring		

3 Now complete the diagram for you.

	easy	difficult
interesting		
boring		

Word Bank

Classifying words helps you to understand and remember them.

Copy this diagram into your notebook and write the subjects in the right place.

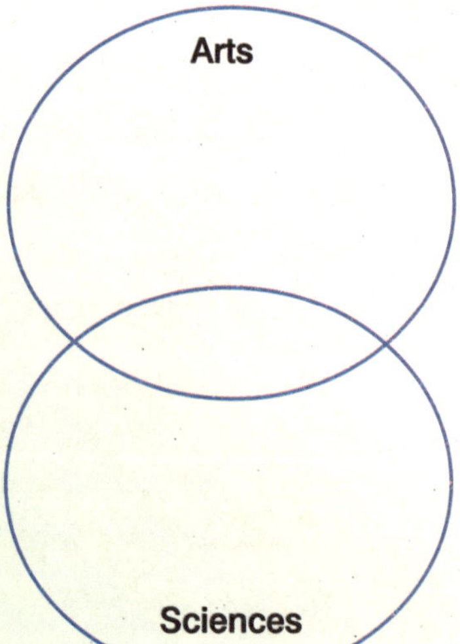

B Function Lending and borrowing

1 Match the words and the photos *a–d*.

English textbook [d] money [ ] MP3 player [ ] pencil [ ]

a

b

c
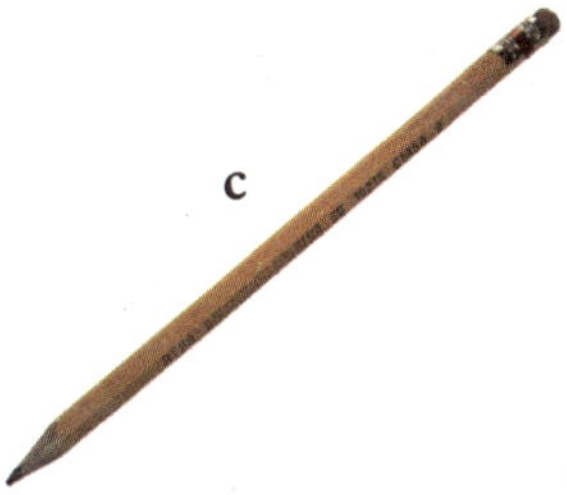

d

2 Listen to Track 63 and match the four dialogues and the photos *a–d* in Activity 1.

Dialogue 1 [d] Dialogue 2 [ ] Dialogue 3 [ ] Dialogue 4 [ ]

3 Listen to Track 63 again and match the question with the reply.

Asking

1 Can I borrow your book? [d]
2 Can you lend me a pencil? [ ]
3 Can you lend me some money? [ ]
4 Can I borrow your MP3 player? [ ]

Answering

a Sorry. I don't have any.
b Sorry. I'm using it.
c Sure. Have this one.
d OK. Here you are.

Just note

lend and *borrow*
lend = give something to someone
borrow = take something from someone

4 Read these sentences and choose the correct form.

a Can you lend / borrow me a book?
b Can I lend / borrow a pencil?
c Can I lend / borrow your car?
d Can you lend / borrow me a jacket?

5 Now match them with the correct answer.

1 Sorry. I have to drive my grandmother to the shops. [c]
2 Sure. I have a sweater I can wear. [ ]
3 OK. This one is great – it's a really interesting story. [ ]
4 Sorry. I only have one and I'm using it. [ ]

Now listen to Track 64 and check your answers.

6 Listen to Track 65 and speak after the beep.

UNIT 17

A Vocabulary Animals

1 Look at the photos and write the names of the animals.

a tac cat..........

b gdo d..........

c bitarb r..........

d somue m..........

e niol l..........

f giret t..........

g tar r..........

h sehro h..........

i ranogako k..........

j rigefaf g..........

k sororhneic r..........

l tanepehl e..........

Now listen to Track 66 and check your answers.

2 Find the names of animals in this puzzle.

agiraffeimousehorabbitacattiregdogandrhinocerostratankangaroothehorseseselephants

3 Complete these sentences with the name of an animal.

a A ....lion....... is often called the king of the jungle.

b .... only live in Australia.

c .... and .... are very common pets.

d .... like eating carrots.

e There are African and Indian ....

f A .... has a very long neck.

Word Bank

Spider diagrams are useful because you can add more words when you need to.

In your notebook, make a spider diagram about animals.

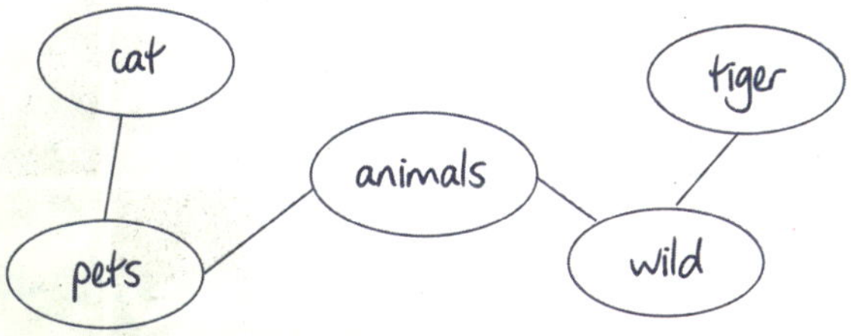

B Function Warnings

1 What is the problem in pictures *a–d*? Listen to Track 67 and match the dialogues with the pictures.

a [3]

b [ ]

c [ ]

d [ ]

2 Listen to Track 67 again and complete the warnings.

1 ....Be....... careful! .... fall in the water!
2 .... out! There's a squirrel on the table.
3 .... the chewing gum.
4 .... touch that bird!

3 Complete the warnings for these pictures. Match the warning to the picture.

1 ....Keep.... off the grass! [b]

2 .... the dog! [ ]

3 .... out! There's a mouse under the table. [ ]

4 .... touch that! [ ]

Now listen to Track 68 and check your answers.

4 Look at the pictures *a–d* in Activity 3. Write one different way to give each warning.

a Look out! It's fragile.

b ....

c ....

d ....

5 Listen to Track 69 and give the warnings as in Activity 4. Speak after the beep.

6 Look at the pictures. How many different ways can you give warnings?

....

....

....

....

....

....

a

b

c

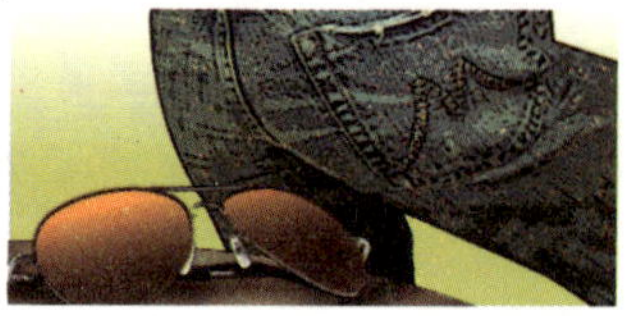

d

UNIT 18

A Vocabulary Weather and seasons

1 Match the words below with the symbols *1–6*.

clouds	ice	rain	snow	sun	wind

1 ......rain......

2 ....

3 ....

4 ....

5 ....

6 ....

2 What's the weather like? Draw the symbol next to the phrase.

a It's raining. 

b It's sunny.

c It's cloudy.

d It's hot.

e It's cold.

f It's snowing.

g It's windy.

h It's icy.

i It's warm.

Listen to Track 70 and check your answers.

3 Look at the names of the seasons.

spring	summer	autumn	winter

What is the weather like in these countries?

a the UK ....

b Australia ....

c Iceland ....

Example: In the UK in the spring, it usually rains a lot, but it is sometimes sunny ...

Now listen to Track 71 and check your answers.

Word Bank

Drawing symbols can help you to remember the words.

In your notebook, write the seasons and the kinds of weather in your country, and add symbols.

spring – rainy 
summer
autumn
winter

4 **What's the weather like in these pictures?**

a It's windy and it's ...

b ....

c ....

5 **Do this crossword.**

1 When is the weather usually hot?
2 When do flowers start to grow?
3 When is it often cold?
4 When do the leaves fall from the trees?

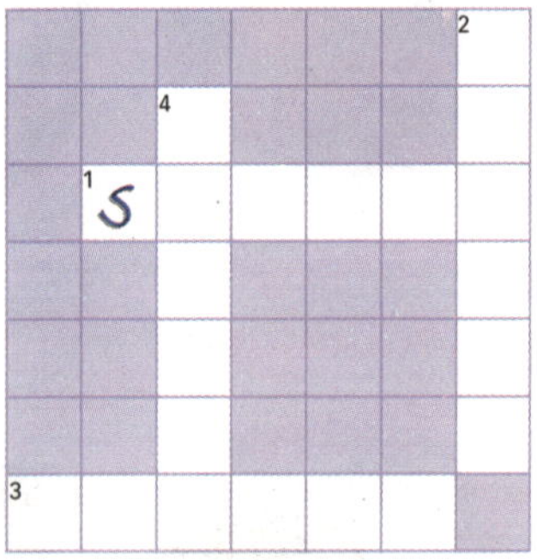

B Function Expressing approval and disapproval

1 **Look at this conversation and number the lines in the right order.**

a Oh no! I hate new shoes too. [ ]
b Yes, they're lovely, but I don't like wearing new shoes. [ ]
c You poor thing! [ ]
d Hello Mrs Brown! How are you? [1]
e Oh, yesterday we were at my nephew's wedding. [ ]
f I was happy to be home to take my shoes off. It was awful! [ ]
g I'm fine, thanks, dear. Where were you yesterday? [ ]
h That's great! I love weddings. [ ]

Listen to Track 72 and check your answers.

2 **Now listen to Track 72 again and put these words in the right place in the table.**

awful lovely great love hate

Expressing approval			Expressing disapproval		
That It	's was	(a) .... ! (b) .... !	That It	's was	(d) .... ! terrible!
I (c) .... I like		(weddings / the rain).	I (e) .... I don't like		(weddings / the rain).

3 **Write what you like and don't like about these things.**

a your school / college / job

....

....

....

b your house

....

....

....

c television

....

....

....

4 **Match the two parts of the conversation.**

a Do you like snow?	1 Yes, it's lovely.
b Do you like cloudy weather?	2 I don't. I hate hot weather.
c I love the sunshine.	3 Oh really? I don't. It's awful.
d I love the rain.	4 No, I hate cold weather.

Now listen to Track 73 and check your answers.

5 **Complete this conversation. Agree or disagree.**

I love watching TV. It's great!

YOU (**a**) ....

Oh really? What about sports? Do you like sports?

YOU (**b**) ....

That's interesting.
Do you want to go out in the rain? Do you like the rain?

YOU (**c**) ....

OK. What about hot weather? Do you like it?

YOU (**d**) ....

Now listen to Track 74 and speak after the beep.

UNIT 19

A Vocabulary Dates and historical events

1 Listen to these dates on Track 75. Label the dates *a–g* as you hear them.

1789 [a]   1947 [ ]   2006 [ ]   1865 [ ]   1861 [ ]   1509 [ ]   1547 [ ]

Repeat the dates.

2 Write the dates of the historical events. Use dates from Activity 1.

a the American Civil War: .... to ....

b the French Revolution: ....

c King Henry VIII: .... to ....

d India's independence: ....

Listen to Track 76 and check your answers.

3 In which of pictures *a–d* above can you see ... ?

1 a soldier [a]

2 a king [ ][ ]

3 a queen [ ][ ]

4 a war [ ]

5 a prime minister [ ]

6 a president [ ]

Word Bank

Writing examples helps you to remember words.

In your notebook, write examples that you know for these words.

a king – King Abdullah II

a queen

a president

a prime minister

a war

a revolution

a soldier

4 Write the dates.

a 1914 ......nineteen fourteen......
b 1945 ....
c 1947 ....
d 1952 ....
e 1963 ....

5 Fill in the blanks with words from the box and the dates in Activity 4.

President	queen	World	Prime Minister	War

a Elizabeth II became ....queen.... of the United Kingdom of Great Britain and Northern Ireland in ....
b Nehru became the first .... of independent India in ....
c World .... I started in ....
d .... War II ended in ....
e .... is the year of the assassination of .... John F. Kennedy.

B Function Telling a story

1 Listen to Sandra and Carl's story on Track 77. Number the actions *a–d* in the order you hear them.

a put make-up on [ ]
b practised the gladiator scene [ ]
c got costumes [1]
d filmed a bit of the crowd [ ]

2 Listen to Track 77 again. Complete the table.

Asking about a sequence of events	Sequence markers
What happened first?	First
Then what happened?	(b) ....
(a) .... ?	(c) ....
	(d) ....
	After that …

3 Work out the order of the pictures. Write *first*, *then*, *next*, *finally* and *after that* in the spaces. Use the sentences in the correct order in the story of Yuri Gagarin in Activity 4.

a

Yuri flew around the Earth.

b

Yuri worked in a steel factory.

c

He trained to become a cosmonaut.

d

He became a pilot in the Russian air force.

e

He took flying lessons as a hobby.

4 Write the story of Yuri Gagarin's career.

Yuri Gagarin was from Russia. He was the world's first cosmonaut. These are some important events in his life. First,

....

....

....

....

....

....

The flight took only 1 hour and 48 minutes. Yuri Gagarin died in 1968 when his plane crashed.

5 Talk to a friend about Yuri Gagarin.

YOUR FRIEND: Who was Yuri Gagarin?

YOU: (**a**) He was the world's first cosmonaut.

YOUR FRIEND: What do you know about his career?

YOU: Well, (**b**) ....

....

YOUR FRIEND: Wow! What happened after that? Did he go round the Earth again?

YOU: (**c**) ....

YOUR FRIEND: Oh no! That's sad.

Listen to Track 78 and speak after the beep.

UNIT 20

A Vocabulary Transport

1 Match these words with these symbols.

bus underground taxi (on) foot train boat bike car

a taxi b .... c .... d .... e .... f .... g .... h ....

2 Match the sections in the brochure below with the symbols *a–h* in Activity 1.

Getting around in London

By underground	The 'tube' is easy and comfortable. There is a station every few streets. Buy a Travelcard to travel after 9.30 a.m. Underground trains run from 5.30 a.m. to 12.00 midnight.	[h]
By bus	Travelling by bus is a good way to see the city, especially from the top of a double-decker. There is always a bus stop nearby. There are special fares for children.	[ ]
By train	Take a train to visit places outside London, like Hampton Court and Windsor Castle. You can use a Travelcard on the tube, buses and most trains. Get a map from railway stations to plan your journey.	[ ]
By taxi	London's famous black taxis are expensive but they are good and comfortable. Take a taxi once, for the experience.	[ ]
By boat	The 'river bus' leaves from Westminster Pier and stops at different places between Westminster and Greenwich Pier. A good way to see the city from the River Thames.	[ ]
By car	Don't drive your car in London. Car parks are very expensive. You have to pay a special congestion charge to drive your car into the centre.	[ ]
By bike	There aren't many safe bicycle lanes in London. Cycling with a large guided group is safer.	[ ]
On foot	The best way to visit the city! But look right and left before you cross a street.	[ ]

Now listen to Track 79 and check your answers.

3 Find the answers in the brochure.

a Where do you wait for the bus?

At a bus stop.

b Where can you take a boat?

c Where can you take a train?

d What time is the first train on the underground?

e Where can you ride a bike safely?

f What's the best way to see London?

g Where can you park your car?

h What is the most comfortable way to see London?

4 Look at the grid carefully. Find and circle:

a nine types of transport
b three verbs related to travel
c two things which are useful for travelling

Use three different colours.

C	O	N	V	E	R	T	I	B	L	E
A	B	I	C	D	E	I	F	G	H	M
R	I	A	J	K	L	C	M	N	R	O
A	O	R	P	B	I	K	E	Q	I	T
V	R	T	S	U	T	E	U	V	D	O
A	W	X	Y	S	Z	T	U	B	E	R
N	A	E	I	O	U	P	L	A	N	H
J	D	R	I	V	E	A	V	I	M	O
I	K	E	C	A	F	L	E	P	A	M
S	P	A	A	L	L	P	L	A	N	E
F	O	U	R	B	Y	F	O	U	R	E

Word Bank

Writing examples helps you to understand and remember words.

In your notebook, write an example of where you would go with these types of transport.

by plane – to the USA	by train
by car – to the shops	by boat
on foot – to school	by bike
by bus	by taxi

B Function Ending a conversation

1 Complete the conversations *a–d* on page 53 with words from the table.

Ending a conversation	
It was nice to talk to you.	I have to go now.
Bye (now / then).	Good night.
Goodbye.	See you (soon / later / around).

Then listen to Track 80 and check your answers.

2 **Put the sentences in the right order to make a conversation.**

a Well, I have to go. It was nice to talk to you. [ ]
b Hi! How's it going? [1]
c You too. See you around. [ ]
d Fine, thanks. You? [ ]
e Great. Did you have a good holiday? [ ]
f Yes, bye. [ ]
g Yes, we did. It was fun. [ ]

Listen to Track 81 and check your answers.

3 **Follow the instructions to complete the dialogue. Then listen to Track 82 and speak after the beep.**

Greet your friend.

YOU: (a) Hi! How's it going?
YOUR FRIEND: Fine, thanks.

Ask about your friend's family.

YOU: (b) .... ?
YOUR FRIEND: Yes, thank you. Everybody's fine. What about your family?

Answer the question. End the conversation.

YOU: (c) ....
YOUR FRIEND: Nice to see you too. Let's get together some time.

Agree. Promise to phone.

YOU: (d) ....
YOUR FRIEND: Yes, give me a call.

Say goodbye.

YOU: (e) ....
YOUR FRIEND: Bye. See you soon.

A Vocabulary Geography

beach (x2) cave cliffs forest mountains river village

1 Correct the labels on the map.

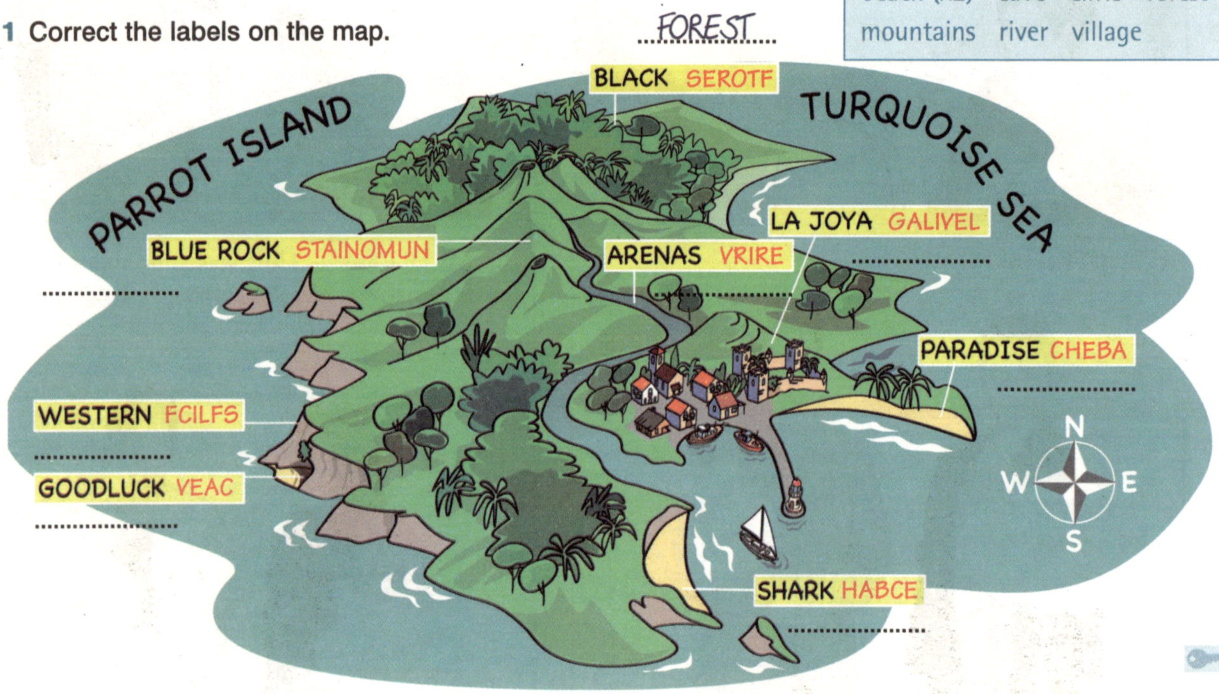

2 Listen to Track 83. Is there treasure on the island? Mark the place on the map with a cross.

3 Listen to Track 84. Match the conversations with the pictures.

Now label the pictures with the words in the box.

beach cave cliffs forest island mountain river sea village

a [ ]

b [ ]

Word Bank

Writing examples can help you remember new words better.

Find words related to geography. Write the words with an example in your notebook.

beach – Miami Beach

island – Hawaii

B Function Expressing hope

1 Write the best caption in the bubble.

a I hope she comes!
b I hope she doesn't come!
c I hope she comes on time!

2 Match the questions with the answers.

Questions	Expressing hope
1 Do you think (that)* you're going to get the job?	**a** Well, they are the best team. *Keep your fingers crossed*!
2 Do you think (that)* it's going to rain?	**b** *I hope so!* I really want that job!
3 Are Liverpool going to win the Cup this year?	**c** On 2nd May. *I hope (that)* you can come!*
4 So when are you getting married?	**d** Well, *I hope (that)* I have enough money*.
5 Are you going to buy that new car?	**e** *I hope not*. We're having a party in the garden.

Listen to Track 85 and check your answers.

Just note
* After verbs like *think* and *hope*, you can leave out *that*.

3 Complete these sentences with *I hope*, *I hope so* or *I hope not*.

a LYDIA: Is Judy coming to the party?
BOBBY: .... I don't like her.

b MARIA: Are you going on holiday?
RACHEL: Well, ... my boss will give me time off.

c SANDY: When is the party?
RICK: Tonight. .... we'll be ready in time.

d JAKE: Is it going to rain?
JANE: .... I want to go for a walk.

e LENNY: Are you going to sing at the wedding?
KERRY: .... , but they haven't asked me yet.

4 Match the questions with the answers. Then write true answers for yourself.

a Is this going to be a good year for you? [3]
b Is it going to rain this afternoon? [ ]
c What are you going to do next weekend? [ ]
d Where are you travelling this year? [ ]

1 I hope (that) I can go to New York. [ ]
2 I hope (that) I have time to go shopping. [ ]
3 I hope so! Keep your fingers crossed! [ ]
4 I hope not. I want to play tennis. [ ]

Write your true answers here.

Is this going to be a good year for you?

....

Is it going to rain this afternoon?

....

What are you going to do next weekend?

....

Where are you travelling this year?

....

5 Write responses.

I have a stomach ache.

YOU: (a) I hope you feel better soon.

I have an English test tomorrow.

YOU: (b) ....

Thank you very much for my present.

YOU: (c) ....

We're going to visit your country!

YOU: (d) ....

We're going to be there in July. Is it going to rain, do you think?

YOU: (e) ....

Do you think we're going to like the food?

YOU: (f) ....

Listen to Track 86 and speak after the beep.

A Vocabulary Places to go

1 Correct the labels. (The first one is done for you.)

a ......theatre......
b ....
c ....
d ....
e ....
f ....
g ....
h ....

a treetha

b simadut

c gealyrl

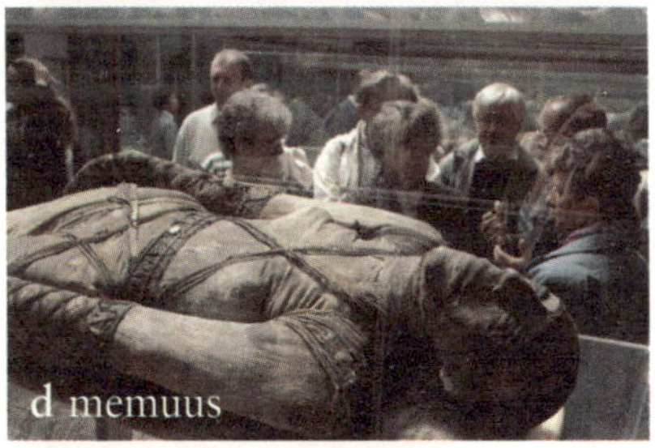
d memuus

e raneustrat

f chelantcrol

g culb

h cemain

2 Where are the people going? Write the names of the places.

cinema	club	concert hall
gallery	museum	restaurant
stadium	theatre	

a 'I'm going to see a movie.' ......cinema......
b 'We're going to eat out. Do you want to come?' ....
c 'We're going clubbing on Saturday.' ....
d 'Bob's taking the kids to see the Egyptian mummies.' ....
e 'We're going to listen to the Symphony Orchestra!' ....
f 'Are you going to the England v Germany match?' ....
g 'I'm going to see a Shakespeare play tonight.' ....
h 'Jill and Jim are going to a photograph exhibition.' ....

Now listen to Track 87 and check your answers.

3 Match the columns to make sentences. Write your sentences.

I want to go to	the cinema a gallery the theatre the stadium a restaurant the museum the concert hall	to have to listen to to see to watch	a film. a match. a famous pianist. a meal. an exhibition. some photographs. a play.

Example: I want to go to the cinema to see / watch a film.

a ...

b ...

c ...

d ...

e ...

f ...

g ...

h ...

i ...

Word Bank

Grouping words together helps you to remember them.

Copy the table into your notebook and complete it.

art classical music club concert hall dance gallery go clubbing have a meal menu museum opera paintings pop music portraits restaurant sculpture

Entertainment			
Eating out	**Music / Dance**	**Exhibitions**	**Clubbing**
restaurant			

B Function Making plans

1 Listen to three conversations on Track 88. What are the people's plans? Make true sentences.

Tessa and Will Jake and Meera Anne and Oliver	are going to	a concert a restaurant stay at home the theatre an exhibition the cinema a cafeteria	on Saturday. on Sunday. today.

Example: 1 Tessa and Will are going to an ...

2 Listen to Track 88 again. Who says these things? Write the names.

Asking about plans	Giving ideas	Accepting
a What are we going to do today? Will	**d** Why don't we go to the cinema?	**i** That sounds interesting. ....
b What shall we do on Saturday?	**e** Let's go to an exhibition.	**j** Let's do that. ....
c What are your plans for Saturday night?	**f** Why don't we watch the match?	**k** What a great idea! ....
	g I've got two tickets for the theatre.	**l** Hmm, I suppose. ....
	h Shall we go to that nice Italian restaurant afterwards?	**m** I'd love to come. ....

3 Number the sentences *1–8* to make a conversation.

What shall we do on Saturday? [1]
That's a good idea. [ ]
There's a Japanese film on at the local cinema. [ ]
Shall I go and buy the tickets? [ ]
That sounds interesting. Let's do that. [ ]
Is there anything good on? [ ]
Why don't we go to the cinema? [ ]
You don't have to go and buy the tickets. You can buy them on the phone. [ ]

Listen to Track 89 and check your answers.

4 Talk to Irina about your weekend plans. Write your responses.

IRINA: Wow! It's the weekend, finally! What are you going to do tomorrow?

YOU: (a) I'm going to... .

IRINA: That sounds good. What are your plans for Sunday?

YOU: (b) ....

What about you?

IRINA: I'm going to go to a pop concert.

YOU: (c) ....

IRINA: Shall we talk again next week?

YOU: (d) ....

IRINA: Well, have a good weekend!

YOU: (e) ....

Listen to Track 90 and speak after the beep.

UNIT 23

A Vocabulary Adjectives

1 Label the pictures with adjectives from the box.

beautiful	handsome	high	long	narrow	tall	thick	thin

Listen to Track 91 and check your answers.

2 Write the opposite adjectives. You need one of the adjectives from the box on the right twice.

cheap	fat	low	old-fashioned	plain	wide	short	thin	unattractive

a beautiful ......plain......
b expensive ....
c handsome ....
d high ....
e long ....
f modern ....
g narrow ....
h tall ....
i thick ....
j thin ....

Just note

1 The CD is *quite* expensive.
2 The CD is *very* expensive.
The CD in 2 is more expensive than the CD in 1.

Complete the sentences with an adjective.

1 The Mississippi is a very ......wide...... river.
2 My MP3 player was only £10. It was very .... because I bought it second hand.
3 Emma isn't .... She eats well and exercises a lot.
4 I prefer .... clothes to fashionable clothes.
5 Jane is quite .... but she has a great personality.
6 The buildings in our town are quite .... There are no tall buildings at all.
7 I don't think Salman is .... , I think he's quite handsome.
8 The maths book is .... but the dictionary is very thick.
9 Jimmy is quite .... for his age: everyone in his class is taller.
10 'Jo' is a very .... name.

3 Complete the sentences with the opposite of the adjectives in brackets.

a This car is very ...cheap... . (expensive)
b My cousin wears very .... clothes. (modern)
c Juan is quite .... (handsome)
d The roads in this city are very .... (narrow)
e Frankly, I think Joanne is quite .... (beautiful)
f The walls around the garden are quite .... (high)
g I have to go on a diet. I'm getting a bit .... (thin)

Word Bank

Writing words with their opposites (antonyms) will help you to remember them.

Write phrases with adjectives from this unit in your notebook and add an antonym.

a cheap book –
an expensive book

4 Circle the adjectives that can go with the nouns. There can be more than one.

a Our *school building* is short / low / handsome / attractive.
b *Martin* is beautiful / high / tall / attractive.
c *The mountains* are tall / high / short / beautiful.
d *This jacket* is too old-fashioned / low / short / long.
e *Maya's* very handsome / beautiful / attractive.

B Function Comparing things

1 Listen to Track 92. What are the sentences about? Write the name of the objects in the table.

dinner service
toaster
DVD recorder

Comparing things	
a It isn't *big enough*. ...dinner service...	**f** It's *much more expensive*. ....
b It's *big enough* for now.	**g** Let's buy the *smaller one*. ....
c It's really *too expensive*.	**h** We need a *bigger one*. ....
d Is that *cheap enough*?	**i** Let's look at *more exciting things* now. ....
e Isn't that *good enough*?	**j** A recorder is *better than* a player. ....

2 Use *not ... enough* or *too* ... and the adjectives in brackets to write sentences.

a four spoonfuls of sugar in a cup of coffee (sweet) ...The coffee is too sweet....
b a one-bedroom flat for a family of six (small) ....
c The jacket is size 10. You are size 14. (big) ....
d The shoes are £80. You've got £60. (expensive) ....
e The film lasts four hours! (long) ....
f The bridge is 2.40 m high, the caravan is 2.50 m high. (high) ....
g The boy is only 1.20 m. The shelf is two metres high. (tall) ....

3 **Listen to Ella and Jesper on Track 93 discussing their plans for a party. What does Ella think of these things? Use the phrases in the boxes.**

too	big spicy hot small soon boring	(not)	big exciting large	enough	cooler better

a the beach It's too hot.

b the house ……

c the garden ……

d Indian food ……

e Italian food ……

f a barbecue ……

g sending invitations ……

Where are they going to have the party? What are they going to eat?

They are going to have the party in the garden.

……

4 **You are going out with a friend. Choose the idea you like best. Give reasons for not accepting his ideas. Use *too*, *enough*, *not enough* or a comparative adjective.**

YOUR FRIEND: What kind of movie do you want to see, a romantic comedy, a western or an action film?

Example: Let's see a romantic comedy. Westerns and action films are too boring.

YOU: (**a**) ……

YOUR FRIEND: What time shall we go, at 2 p.m., 6 p.m. or 10 p.m.?

YOU: (**b**) ……

YOUR FRIEND: Shall we go to a restaurant after?

YOU: (**c**) ……

YOUR FRIEND: OK. Do you want to walk or take a taxi? Or shall we take our bikes?

YOU: (**d**) ……

YOUR FRIEND: OK. See you later.

Listen to Track 94 and speak after the beep.

UNIT 24

A Vocabulary Technology

1 Match the items on the left with the words on the right.

a Blackberry™ [4] b plasma screen [ ] c digital camera [ ]	1 photography
d laptop [ ] e memory stick [ ] f cordless phone [ ]	2 computers
g DVD recorder [ ] h high definition [ ]	3 television
	4 communication

Now listen to Track 95 and check your answers.

2 Answer the questions about the advertisements below.

Which gadget ...

a is a camera? ....
b records and stores television programmes? ....
c stores songs? ....
d has a hard disk, like a computer? ....
e is good for listening to the radio? ....
f can do your cleaning? ....
g can you phone? ....
h can you take with you? ....
i needs a special card, like a mobile phone? ....

The future is here.

And it's at Galaxy, your technology store!

Eyesee
What happens in your house when you are not there? Eyesee is a camera with a mobile phone card inside. Make a video call to Eyesee on your mobile and you can see what's happening.

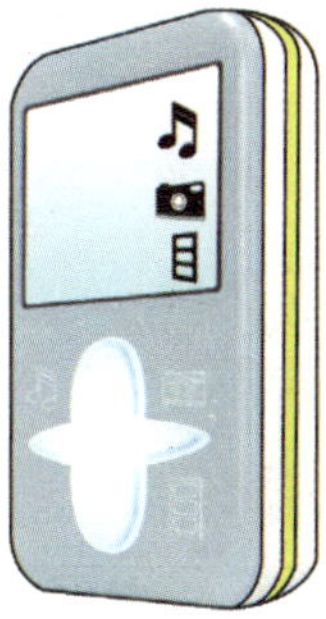

Nomad
You've got to have this portable personal video player. The hard disk of the Nomad holds 100 hours of video or 12,000 songs. It has a 2.5-inch screen. Listen to FM radio and record your programme too!

Robbie the Robot
Robbie the Robot can clean all your floors so you can relax. It can even clean under furniture. Turn it on when you go out and come home to a clean house.

Sonic tmx-402 DVD recorder
The Sonic tmx-402 has a large hard disk and includes a DVD recorder. Big enough for 400 hours of television. When that's full, you can copy and store the contents onto a DVD.

3 What is it? Write the name of the gadgets from Activity 1 in the spaces.

a It's a camera. It doesn't need any film.

a d*igital*........ c*amera*........

b It's a screen. It is flat. You can hang it on the wall. a p.................. s..................

c It's small. You can put it on your knees. It's a computer. a l.................. c..................

d It's a telephone. You normally use it at home. It has no wires.

a c.................. p..................

e It can go in your pocket. It has many buttons. It has email and Internet connection.

a B..................

f It records programmes. It uses DVDs. It can have a hard disk.

a D.................. r..................

g It's only about 6 cm. It's plastic. It stores computer documents.

a m.................. s..................

h It's a television. It's quite new. It has a fantastic picture.

a h.................. d.................. t..................

4 Which of the things in Activity 3 are good for these actions? Write the name.

a take photos: *digital camera*..................

b watch TV: ....

c email: ....

d work on planes: ....

e save your work: ....

f phone from the garden: ....

Word Bank

Making spider diagrams helps you to connect related words.

Copy this diagram into your notebook and complete it with technology words. Write the words for the items you have in one colour, the words for the items you don't have in another colour.

photography — *digital camera*

communication

television — *plasma screen*

computers

B Function Asking for and giving opinions

1 Listen to a discussion on Track 96. Who says these things? Write *Dave* or *Beth* next to sentences *a–d*.

a Anything that makes life better is important. Don't you agree? *Beth*

b A robot is not going to make your life better, not really. ....

c What new technology would you like to have? ....

d Now that's great technology! ....

2 Listen to Track 96 again. What do Dave and Beth say when they ask for and give opinions? Write the phrases in the table.

Asking for opinions	Giving opinions
Do you agree (with me)? (a) .... ?	That's right. (b) .... (c) ....
	That's wrong. (d) .... (e) ....

3 Match the opinions and the responses.

Opinions

a Older people can't use technology. [4]
b I think technology is important in medicine. [ ]
c The world is better thanks to technology. Don't you agree? [ ]
d Old people hate computers. [ ]
e A BlackberryTM is better than a mobile phone. [ ]

Responses

1 That's right. It is a better place.
2 I agree but it is important for other things too.
3 You're right, but it's more expensive.
4 You're wrong. Anyone can learn.
5 I don't agree. My grandmother emails her friends.

4 Respond to these people's opinions. Give reasons.

I think robots that clean the house are a really good idea. What do you think?

YOU: (a) That's wrong. Robots are a silly idea.

Computers are better than people. They don't make mistakes. Don't you agree?

YOU: (b) ....

Big, fast cars in big cities are a really bad idea. Don't you think?

YOU: (c) ....

I think cycling is better than driving. Do you agree with me?

YOU: (d) ....

Space travel doesn't do anything good for people.

YOU: (e) ....

Listen to this in the paper: 'Computer games are bad for children.' Do you agree with that?

YOU: (f) ....

Now listen to Track 97 and speak after the beep.

AUDIOSCRIPTS

CD 1

Track 1

a WOMAN: Wow! Thank you!
MAN: That's OK.
b WOMAN: Ouch!
MAN: Oops! Sorry!
c MAN: Well, see you later!
WOMAN: Yes. Bye!
d WOMAN 1: Excuse me. Excuse me.
WOMAN 2: Yes?
WOMAN 1: Is this the bus to Piccadilly?
e MAN 1: Do you know what time the cafeteria closes?
MAN 2: Sorry?
f WOMAN: ...
WOMAN: I don't understand.

Track 2

a MAN: Sorry!
WOMAN: Sorry!
b WOMAN: Thank you.
MAN: That's OK.
c MAN: I don't understand.
d WOMAN: Excuse me! Excuse me!
e TEACHER: Question 4. Bobby?
BOBBY: Sorry?

Track 3

STEVE: Hello, I'm Steve.
JANIE: Hi Steve. How are you? I'm Janie.
STEVE: Janie, this is Françoise.
JANIE: Nice to meet you, Françoise.
FRANÇOISE: Nice to meet you too.

MAN 1: Good morning, Ms Peters.
MS PETERS: Good morning.
MAN 1: This is Mr Watanabe.
MS PETERS: Pleased to meet you, Mr Watanabe.
MR WATANABE: Pleased to meet you too, Ms Peters.

Track 4

a WOMAN 1: Hi! I'm from France.
b MAN 1: Hello. I'm from South Africa.
c WOMAN 2: Hi. I'm from China.
d MAN 2: Hello. I'm from Mexico.
e WOMAN 3: Hello. I'm from Russia.
f MAN 3: I'm from Korea.

Track 5

Hi! My name's Sue. I'm Canadian.
Hello! I'm Brazilian. My name's Milton.
G'Day. I'm Miranda. I'm Australian.
Hello. My name's Ken and I'm Japanese.
Hello. I'm British. My name's Karen.
Hi. I'm Ed. I'm American.

Track 6

1
MR JOHNSON: Good afternoon.
BANK MANAGER: Good afternoon, Mr Johnson. How are you?
MR JOHNSON: I'm very well, thank you. And you?
BANK MANAGER: Fine, thank you.
2
DOORMAN: Good evening.
WOMAN: Hello.
DOORMAN: How are you?
WOMAN: Fine, thank you.
3
MAN 1: Hello Marty.
MARTY: Hi!
MAN 1: How's it going?
MARTY: Not bad, thanks. You?
MAN 1: Fine, thanks.

Track 7

a I'm an actor.
b Hi! I'm Ben Lomax and I'm a taxi driver.
c Hello. My name's Lucy Barnes and I'm an architect.
d My name's Julie and I'm a singer.
e I'm a student at York university.
f I'm a cleaner.
g Come this way. I'm Nurse Jenkins.
h OK everyone. My name's Mr Jarred and I'm your new teacher.
i Let me through. I'm a doctor.
j My name's James Murray and I'm an engineer.
k Can I help you? I'm an accountant.
l What do you want for dinner? I'm a cook.

Track 8

MARSHALL: Hi! I'm Marshall.
LINDA: Nice to meet you, Marshall. I'm Linda.
MARSHALL: What do you do?
LINDA: I'm a nurse.
MARSHALL: That's great.
LINDA: What do you do?
MARSHALL: I'm an actor.
LINDA: Oh, that's interesting.

MARIE: Hello. I'm Marie.
RICHARD: Hello. I'm Richard. Nice to meet you.
MARIE: What's your job, Richard?
RICHARD: I'm a cleaner here.
MARIE: Oh, really?
RICHARD: Yes. What do you do?
MARIE: I'm a cook.
RICHARD: That's interesting.

Track 9

LUCIA: Oh hello! Meet the family. First, there's Bob and Mike – they're brothers. Kirsty and Pippa are sisters. Then, Bob and Leyla are husband and wife and Tim and Pippa are cousins. Now, Keiko and Mike are Tim and Tom's mother and father and Bob and Leyla have four children: two sons and two daughters. I'm Lucia. I'm a happy grandmother. I have seven grandchildren – four grandsons and three granddaughters and all the children have one uncle and one aunt. Aren't they lovely?

Track 10

one
two
three
four
five
six
seven
eight
nine
ten
eleven
twelve
thirteen
fourteen
fifteen
sixteen
seventeen
eighteen
nineteen
twenty
thirty
forty
fifty
sixty
seventy
eighty
ninety
a hundred

Track 11

1 GIRL 1: Oh, your dog is lovely! What's its name?
GIRL 2: Chaplin.
GIRL 1: How old is it?
GIRL 2: Three months old.

2 BOY: One ticket, please.
MAN: How old are you?
BOY: Fifteen. No, I mean, 18.

3 WOMAN: Look, this is Mrs Johnson, my teacher at school.
MAN: How old is she?
WOMAN: She's 100 years old today!

4 WOMAN 1: Happy birthday, Lara! How old are you today?
LARA: I'm 50-something. Oh, all right, I'm 55.
WOMAN 1: Fifty-five years old! No, you look about 30!

Track 12

a I always have breakfast.
b Hmm. It's lovely to have a shower in the mornings.
c Ahhh. It's great to relax.
d I'm ready to go to bed.
e I have to go to work every day.
f I hate to get up early.
g Hmm. Great. I have a few minutes to read the paper.
h OK. Time to watch television.
i Joe likes to sleep eight hours every night.
j Oh no! I have to work late again tonight.

Track 13

1
ANCHORMAN: It's 12 o'clock. The news on this Thursday the 25th of October. This morning, the Prime Minister ...
2
MAN: Excuse me. Do you have the time please?
WOMAN: Sorry?
MAN: Do you have the time?
WOMAN: Oh, yes. It's quarter to twelve.
MAN: Quarter to twelve? Thanks.
3
WOMAN 1: What time is your class?
WOMAN 2: What?
WOMAN 1: What time is your class?
WOMAN 2: At half past twelve. What time is it now?
WOMAN 1: It's half past twelve now.
WOMAN 2: Half past twelve! I'm late. Bye.
4
SPEAKING CLOCK: It is now exactly three minutes past twelve.

Track 14

a It's 12 o'clock midday in London. What time is it in San Francisco?
b It's 3.15 p.m. in London. What's the time in Mexico City?
c It's 4.45 a.m. in Buenos Aires. What time is it in Paris?
d It's 6.30 p.m. in Beijing, China. What time is it in Sydney?
e It's 9.03 a.m. in New York. What's the time in São Paulo?
f It's 7.20 p.m. in London. What time is it in your country?

Track 15

WOMAN: What do you like to have for breakfast?
MAN: I like bread and coffee. How about you?

Track 16

STELLA: It's one o'clock – lunchtime! In Britain, we have a small meal at lunch and a big meal in the evening. What about your country?
- I like to have tea, milk and bread for breakfast. And you?
- What about lunch? I like a sandwich and some fruit.
- Dinner is at 7.00. We have meat or fish and vegetables. What about you?

- I like snacks in the afternoon, chocolate for example. How about you?
- Back to work now. Talk to you soon!

Track 17

1

ASSISTANT: Next please.

CUSTOMER: A cheese sandwich and a chocolate cake, please.

ASSISTANT: Coming up. And to drink?

CUSTOMER: Sorry?

ASSISTANT: What would you like to drink?

CUSTOMER: I'll have a cup of tea. Milk, no sugar.

ASSISTANT: Sure. That's £6.25 please.

2

ASSISTANT: Can I help you?

CUSTOMER: I'd like fish and chips and a Coke.

ASSISTANT: Sure. Anything else?

CUSTOMER: Can I have some ketchup, please?

ASSISTANT: Here you are. That's £5.50, please.

CUSTOMER: Thanks.

Track 18

ASSISTANT: Can I help you?

CUSTOMER: I'd like a cheese sandwich and a chocolate ice cream, please.

ASSISTANT: What would you like to drink?

CUSTOMER: I'll have a cup of coffee. Milk, no sugar.

ASSISTANT: Anything else?

CUSTOMER: No thank you.

ASSISTANT: That's £5.20, please.

Track 19

WOMAN: I'll have a chicken salad and a chocolate cake, please.

- I'd like an orange juice.
- That's all, thank you.

Track 20

a Sasha likes travelling.
b Martin likes doing puzzles.
c Jake and Sandra like watching TV.
d Chloe likes playing video games.
e Johanna likes reading.
f Candy likes working out.
g Mark and Patrick like going to the cinema.
h Marie and John like playing sports.
i Karl likes listening to music.
j Sally and Karen like going shopping.

Track 21

a MATT: I love skiing. It's great.
ELLA: I don't think so. It's boring.

b SUSIE: Do you like going to the cinema? I do. I think it's fun.
JOE: I agree. It's fun.

c MAN: Kevin likes playing football.
WOMAN: No, dear. That's not right. He likes playing basketball.

d CHARLIE: Dad likes going shopping, Mum.
MOTHER: Of course he does, Charlie.

e MAN: Bono is English, right?
WOMAN: Certainly not. He's from Ireland. He's Irish.

Track 22

MAN: We love playing football. It's fun.
WOMAN: I agree. It's great fun.

WOMAN: Ronaldinho is Mexican, right?
MAN: Certainly not. He's Brazilian.

MAN: You like going shopping, don't you?
WOMAN: Of course I do.

WOMAN: Susie really likes doing puzzles.
MAN: No, that's not right. She likes reading.

Track 23

a You like travelling, don't you?
b English is fun.
c Shakira is French, right?
d I like Chinese food. It's delicious.
e You like Italian food, right?
f Angelina Jolie is German, isn't she?
g Watching TV is boring.

Track 24

a You use your head to think.
b You use your legs and feet to walk.
c You need your mouth (and your throat) to sing.
d You usually lie down on your back.
e Food goes into your stomach.
f You use your nose to smell.
g You see and hear things with your eyes and ears.
h You eat food with your mouth and your teeth.
i You use your chest (and your nose) to breathe.
j You use your arms and legs to drive a car.

Track 25

1 MAN: What's the matter?
WOMAN: I have a problem.
MAN: Oh, I'm sorry to hear that.

2 MAN: What's wrong?
WOMAN: I've got a cold.
MAN: Oh, you poor thing.

3 WOMAN: What's the matter with James?
MAN: His stomach hurts.
WOMAN: Poor James.

4 WOMAN: What's wrong with Sarah?
MAN: Her back hurts.
WOMAN: Oh dear.

5 WOMAN: How do you feel?
MAN: I feel awful. My throat hurts and my head hurts.
WOMAN: Oh dear. I'm sorry to hear that.

Track 26

a MAN: What's the matter with Janie?
WOMAN: Her throat hurts.
MAN: Poor Janie.

b WOMAN: What's wrong with Billy?
MAN: He's got a problem.
WOMAN: Oh, dear. Poor Billy.

c WOMAN: How do you feel?
MAN: I feel awful. My head hurts.
WOMAN: You poor thing!

Track 27

a MAN: What's the matter with Janie?
– Poor Janie.

b MAN: He's got a problem.

c WOMAN: How do you feel?
– You poor thing!

Track 28

a Oh! What a beautiful dress!
b I need a new suit for work.
c That's a cool pair of trousers.
d Hmm. I'll take that blue shirt.
e That's a great pair of black shoes.
f Nice tie!
g I need a new skirt.
h Cool T-shirt!
i I need a warm sweater.
j I like that jacket!
k Do you have grey socks?

Track 29

a

CUSTOMER: Excuse me. How much is that skirt?
ASSISTANT: It's £25.
CUSTOMER: Do you have a medium?
ASSISTANT: Yes. Do you want to try it?
CUSTOMER: Yes, please.

b

CUSTOMER: I'd like a tie.
ASSISTANT: Yes, of course. What about this one?
CUSTOMER: How much does it cost?
ASSISTANT: £10.
CUSTOMER: Thanks. I'll take it.
ASSISTANT: Here you are. That's £10.
CUSTOMER: Thank you.

Track 30

1

CUSTOMER: Excuse me. How much is this bread?
– I'll take two, please. How much is that?
– No, thank you.

2

ASSISTANT: Certainly. What about this black one?
– £50. Do you want to try it?

Track 31

1

CUSTOMER: Excuse me. How much is this bread?
ASSISTANT: It's £1.50 a loaf.
CUSTOMER: I'll take two, please. How much is that?
ASSISTANT: That's £3.00. Anything else?
CUSTOMER: No, thank you.

2

CUSTOMER: I'd like a dress.
ASSISTANT: Certainly. What about this black one?
CUSTOMER: How much does it cost?
ASSISTANT: £50. Do you want to try it?
CUSTOMER: Yes, please.

Track 32

a When do you drive?
b When do you clap?
c Do you ever fall?
d Do you ever climb?
e Do you ever jump?
f When do you ride?
g When do you cheer?
h Do you ever throw anything?
i How often do you dance?
j Do you ever hit a ball?

Track 33

MAN: Hello! Can I take a minute of your time?
DANIELA: Sorry? I don't understand. Can you speak slowly, please?
MAN: Yes. Have you got time to talk for a minute?
DANIELA: Sure.
MAN: Are you interested in animal welfare?
DANIELA: Sorry. What does 'welfare' mean?
MAN: Welfare? It's, you know, when animals are happy.
DANIELA: Ah yes, of course.
MAN: Well, you know, your contribution can really make a difference.
DANIELA: Can you say that again, please?
MAN: I'm saying, your money can help the animals.
DANIELA: Oh! I'm sorry, I haven't got ... erm ... how do you say 'small money'?
MAN: Small money? Oh, change. You haven't got any change! OK, thanks.
DANIELA: Bye.

Track 34

WOMAN: What does 'clothes' mean?
MAN: Things we wear.
MAN: How do you say 'not very often'?
WOMAN: Occasionally.
WOMAN: What does 'magazine' mean?
MAN: It's something to read and it has a lot of pictures.
MAN: How do you say 'the part of your body where food goes'?
WOMAN: Stomach.

Track 35

JOANNE: Do you want to come to the cinema with us?
KEN: Can you speak more slowly, please?
JOANNE: There's a great movie this evening.
KEN: What does 'movie' mean?
JOANNE: It's a film.
KEN: Can you say that again, please?
JOANNE: A movie is a film at the cinema.

KEN: I'd love to go to the movie!
JOANNE: Great.

Track 36

JOANNE: Do you want to come to the cinema with us?
– There's a great movie this evening.
– It's a film.
– A movie is a film at the cinema.
– Great.

Track 37

chubby, red, wavy, short, long, medium build, fat, slim, grey, blonde, brown, dark, overweight, medium height, curly, green, tall, thin, medium length, black, straight, blue

Track 38

a Larry is short and a bit chubby. He's got long blonde hair and blue eyes.
b Helen is tall and she is a bit overweight. She has long dark hair and dark eyes.

Track 39

MAN: What does Alicia look like?
WOMAN: What does Frank look like?

Track 40

WOMAN: I think I have the perfect model for the fashion show.
MAN: Oh good. How old is she?
WOMAN: Twenty-one.
MAN: What does she look like?
WOMAN: She's got green eyes, long dark hair, very straight. Lovely dark skin. Look, here's her photo.
MAN: Hmm. She looks nice. How tall is she?
WOMAN: One metre 75.
MAN: And how much does she weigh?
WOMAN: Sixty-three kilos. She's very slim.
MAN: Yes, I agree with you. She's perfect for the job.
WOMAN: OK. I'll call her.

Track 41

MARY: Do you know Joe?
FREDDIE: I'm not sure. What does he look like?
MARY: He's got short blonde hair and blue eyes.
FREDDIE: Hmm. How tall is he?
MARY: About 1.85, I think.
FREDDIE: Is he thin? How much does he weigh?
MARY: I don't know. He's slim, maybe about 90 kilos.
FREDDIE: I think I know him. How old is he?
MARY: About 25.
FREDDIE: Oh, yes. I know him. What about him?

Track 42

MAN: I'm not sure. What does she look like?
– Hmm. How tall is she?
– How much does she weigh?
– Yes, I think I know her. How old is she?

Track 43

How often do you send emails?
How often do you send text messages?
How often do you go on the Internet?
How often do you send a fax?
How often do you take photos?
How often do you send photos?
How often do you leave a voice message?
How often do you play games?
How often do you make a phone call?

Track 44

a Sherry talks on the phone for hours!
b Tom likes playing games on the computer.
c Leave Mike a message on his answering machine.
d Find the information on the Internet.
e Call me on my mobile phone.
f Jane always sends her reports by fax.
g I often send photos by email.
h We sometimes order food by phone.

Track 45

1
BOY: Hello?
ROBIN: This is Robin. Can I speak to Jodi, please?
BOY: Sure. Hold on.
Jodi, phone for you! It's Robin.
JODI: I'm not here!
BOY: Sorry, Robin. Jodi says she is not here. Do you want to leave a message?

2
BOY: Hello?
MAN: Can I speak to Jodi Parker please?
BOY: She's at the cinema. Who's speaking?
MAN: It's her manager.
BOY: Oh. Then Jodi's in bed with a cold. Can I take a message?

Track 46

MARIANA: Hello?
FERNANDO: Hello.
MARIANA: Can I speak to Lyndsay, please?
FERNANDO: She's not here. Who's speaking?
MARIANA: It's Mariana.
FERNANDO: Do you want to leave a message?
MARIANA: Yes, please. Can you tell her that Mariana and Robin aren't coming to the party, because Robin is sick.
FERNANDO: Sure, I'll tell her.
MARIANA: Thanks. Bye.
FERNANDO: Bye.

Track 47

MARIANA: Hello?
– Can I speak to Lyndsay, please?
– It's Mariana.
– Yes, please. Can you tell her that Mariana and Robin aren't coming to the party, because Robin is sick.
– Thanks. Bye.

Track 48

Well, in our house we have a sofa and some chairs in the living room, and a lamp. The TV is also in the living room. We have a table and chairs in the dining room. We also have a rug in the dining room and a rug in the living room. In the kitchen there's a stove and a fridge. In the bathroom there's a toilet and a shower, of course. In the bedroom there's a bed (of course) and a desk and a computer … oh, and a chair. There are curtains in every room except the bathroom and the kitchen.

Track 49

a MAN: Have you seen my keys?
WOMAN: Yes, they're on the table near the door.

b BOY: Mum! Where's my shirt?
MOTHER: I don't know. Look in your room. Is it on your bed?
BOY: No, it isn't.
MOTHER: Is it on the chair?
BOY: Oh yes. Here it is.

c WOMAN: Where's the remote control?
MAN: I don't know! Is it on the table?
WOMAN: No, it isn't.
MAN: Is it under that book?
WOMAN: No. Here it is – it's on the TV.

d MAN: Hey Jane. Have you seen my sunglasses?
JANE: No. Are they on the table?
MAN: No, they aren't.
JANE: Are they in the kitchen?
MAN: No.
JANE: Ah, there they are. They're on the computer.

Track 50

1

MAN: Have you seen my watch?
WOMAN: No. Is it under the newspaper?
MAN: Where's the newspaper?
WOMAN: In the living room.
MAN: No, it isn't under the newspaper.
WOMAN: Is it in the bathroom?
MAN: Oh, yes. Here it is.

2

WOMAN: Where are my glasses?
MAN: Are they on the fridge?
WOMAN: No, they aren't in the kitchen.
MAN: Are they in the living room?
WOMAN: Oh, yes, here they are, next to the TV.

CD 2

Track 51

KENNY: Have you seen my keys?
– No, they aren't.
– No.
– Oh, yes. Here they are. Thanks.

Track 52

a MAN: I need to buy a stamp.
WOMAN: Go to the post office.

b WOMAN: I need to change some money.
MAN: You need to go to the bank.

c MAN: I have to go and borrow a book.
WOMAN: Oh. Are you going to the library?

d WOMAN: Let's go for a walk.
MAN: OK. Let's go to the park.

e MAN: Where can we park the car?
WOMAN: There's a car park over here.

f WOMAN: I have to go to a meeting.
MAN: Where? At the town hall?

g WOMAN: It's so hot – let's go swimming.
MAN: Good idea. There's a swimming pool in town.

h MAN: I really need some new shoes.
WOMAN: Come on. I'll take you to the shopping centre.

i WOMAN: I need to see a doctor.
MAN: Why don't you go to the hospital?

j MAN: Fancy a game of squash?
WOMAN: Sure, let's go down to the sports centre.

k WOMAN: We need some eggs.
MAN: I'll go to the supermarket and get some.

l MAN: I have a maths test tomorrow at school.
WOMAN: You poor thing.

m WOMAN: I need to lose weight.
MAN: Why don't you come to the gym with me?

n MAN: Let's go to see a film.
WOMAN: Yes, there are two good ones at the cinema this week.

Track 53

a

MAN: Excuse me. Where's the library?
WOMAN: Go down this street and turn left. The library's on the right next to the post office.
MAN: Thanks.

b

WOMAN: Excuse me. Is there a supermarket near here?
MAN: Hmm. There's one here, on High Street. Go up this street. The supermarket's on the left opposite the cinema.
WOMAN: Thanks.

c

MAN 1: I'm looking for the football tournament, at the sports centre. Is there a sports centre near here?
MAN 2: Yes. Go straight along this street, then turn right at Broad Street and the sports centre is on the left.
MAN 1: Thank you.

Track 54

a MAN: Excuse me, where's the cinema?
WOMAN: Go up High Street and the cinema is on the right.

b WOMAN: Excuse me, is there a post office near here?
MAN: Yes. Go along this street and turn left. The post office is on the right.

c MAN: Excuse me, where's the hospital?
WOMAN: Go up this street and turn right. Go along Broad Street and the hospital is on the left.

d MAN: Excuse me, is there a school near here?
WOMAN: Go up this street and turn left. The school is on the right.

Track 55

MAN: Excuse me, is there a hospital near here?
WOMAN: Yes, dear. Go straight along this street. Turn left onto Green Street and go up the street. The hospital is on the left.

Track 56

a MAN: Excuse me. Where's the library?
– Thank you.
b WOMAN: Excuse me. Is there a supermarket near here?
– Thanks.
c MAN: Excuse me. Where's the cinema?
– Thank you.
d WOMAN: Excuse me. Where's the town hall?
– Thanks.

Track 57

1 piano
2 guitar
3 violin
4 trumpet
5 drums
6 saxophone
7 clarinet

Track 58

1 JOHN: May I leave the room?
MS DAWSON: Of course. But be quick.
2 JUSTIN: Hey Mum, can I turn the TV on?
MOTHER: Not now. We're having dinner.
3 SIMON: Mr Lacey, can I have the day off tomorrow?
MR LACEY: Hmm. We're not busy. Sure.
4 SALLY: Excuse me. Do you mind if I turn the music up?
MARGARET: Of course not.
SALLY: Thank you.

Track 59

a BOY: May I go in?
TEACHER: Sure. Go in and sit down.
b GIRL 1: Do you mind if I play the drums?
GIRL 2: Not now. I want to read.
c GIRL: Can I go out with my friends?
MOTHER: Not tonight, dear. You have school tomorrow.
d MAN: Do you mind if I open the window?
WOMAN: Sure. It's hot in here.

Track 60

a WOMAN: May I turn the music down?
MAN: Yes, of course. It's very loud.
b MAN: Do you mind if I open the window?
WOMAN: No, I don't. Go ahead.
c BOY: Can I go to Joe's party tonight?
MOTHER: No, you can't. You have school tomorrow.
d WOMAN: Do you mind if I watch the TV?
MAN: That's fine. See if there's a good programme.
e MAN: Can I borrow your car?
WOMAN: OK, but I need it this afternoon.
f WOMAN: Can I listen to your CDs?
MAN: Sure. Find something you like.

Track 61

a May I turn the music down?
b No, I don't. Go ahead.
c Can I go to Joe's party tonight?
d That's fine. See if there's a good programme.
e Can I borrow your car?
f Sure. Find something you like.

Track 62

MARTHA: I love going to college – most of the time. I love history – it's interesting and it's pretty easy for me, so is English and so is art. I'm not so good at maths – I like it, it's really interesting, but I find it difficult, and physics I find difficult and boring. Biology and chemistry are interesting, but biology is easy and I find chemistry difficult. Finally, there's PE and geography. They're both boring subjects, but geography is difficult and PE is easy.

Track 63

1 BOY: Can I borrow your book?
GIRL: OK. Here you are.
2 GIRL: Can you lend me a pencil?
BOY: Sure. Have this one.
3 MAN: Can you lend me some money?
WOMAN: Sorry. I don't have any.
4 WOMAN: Can I borrow your MP3 player?
MAN: Sorry. I'm using it.

Track 64

a WOMAN: Can you lend me a book?
MAN: OK. This one is great – it's a really interesting story.
b MAN: Can I borrow a pencil?
WOMAN: Sorry. I only have one and I'm using it.
c WOMAN: Can I borrow your car?
MAN: Sorry. I have to drive my grandmother to the shops.
d MAN: Can you lend me a jacket?
WOMAN: Sure. I have a sweater I can wear.

Track 65

a Can you lend me a book?
b Sorry. I only have one and I'm using it.
c Can I borrow your car?
d Sure. I have a sweater I can wear.

Track 66

a What a pretty cat!
b That's a nice dog.
c Oh! It's a rabbit.
d Ahhhh! A mouse!

e Look at that lion.
f Wow! What a beautiful tiger.
g Yuck! It's a rat.
h What a nice horse.
i Look! A kangaroo!
j Look! There's a giraffe.
k Hey! I can see a rhino – yes, a big rhinoceros.
l Look, an elephant!

Track 67

1 WOMAN: Be careful! Don't fall in the water!
MAN: Aaaaahhh! ...
2 MAN 1: Look out! There's a squirrel on the table.
MAN 2: Go away!
3 MAN: Mind the chewing gum.
WOMAN: Oh, thanks.
4 WARDEN: Don't touch that bird!
WOMAN: Ahhhh.

Track 68

1 Keep off the grass!
2 Mind the dog!
3 Look out! There's a mouse under the table!
4 Don't touch that!

Track 69

a Don't touch that!
b Keep off the grass!
c Look out! There's a mouse under the table!
d Mind the dog!

Track 70

a It's raining! – Picture 1.
b It's sunny – Picture 2.
c It's cloudy – Picture 4.
d Phew! It's hot – Picture 2.
e It's cold – Picture 3 and picture 6.
f It's snowing – Picture 6.
g It's windy – Picture 5.
h It's icy – Picture 3.
i It's warm – Picture 2.

Track 71

a In the UK in the spring, it usually rains a lot, but it is sometimes sunny and warm. In summer, it's usually warm, but sometimes it rains; in autumn, it's sometimes sunny, but it's usually cold and it often rains, and in winter, it's usually cold, it often rains and it sometimes snows.
b In Australia, it depends on the region, but it is often cool in the spring and it often rains. It is usually hot in summer (very hot in some parts). It is cool in autumn and it often rains. In the winter, it is cold and it often snows in the mountains.
c In Iceland, it is cool in the summer and cold in winter. It often rains in summer and always snows in winter.

Track 72

WOMAN: Hello Mrs Brown! How are you?
MRS BROWN: I'm fine, thanks, dear. Where were you yesterday?
WOMAN: Oh, yesterday we were at my nephew's wedding.
MRS BROWN: That's great! I love weddings.
WOMAN: Yes, they're lovely, but I don't like wearing new shoes.
MRS BROWN: Oh no! I hate new shoes too.
WOMAN: I was happy to be home to take my shoes off. It was awful!
MRS BROWN: You poor thing!

Track 73

a MAN: Do you like snow?
WOMAN: No, I hate cold weather.
b MAN: Do you like cloudy weather?
WOMAN: Yes, it's lovely.
c MAN: I love the sunshine.
WOMAN: I don't. I hate hot weather.
d MAN: I love the rain.
WOMAN: Oh really? I don't. It's awful.

Track 74

– I love watching TV. It's great!
– Oh really? What about sports? Do you like sports?
– That's interesting. Do you want to go out in the rain? Do you like the rain?
– OK. What about hot weather? Do you like it?

Track 75

a 1789
b 1509
c 1547
d 1861
e 1865
f 1947
g 2006

Track 76

a
ONLOOKER: Excuse me, what film are you making?
MAN 2: We're making a movie about the American Civil War. I play President Lincoln and my friend here is a Yankee soldier.
ONLOOKER: When was the American Civil War?
MAN 2: From 1861 to 1865.
b
ONLOOKER: Wow! I love your hair! What movie are you making?
WOMAN 2: We're making a film about the French Revolution of 1789. I'm Marie-Antoinette and Bobby da Nero plays my husband, King Louis XVI.
ONLOOKER: Oh, so do they cut your head off?
WOMAN 2: Yes, they behead me at the end of the film!
ONLOOKER: Ouch!

c

ONLOOKER: What's going on? What are those people doing?

MAN: They're making a documentary about English kings and queens. That's Henry VIII and his six wives.

ONLOOKER: Six wives! When was Henry VIII king?

MAN: In the 16th century, from 1509 to 1547.

d

ONLOOKER 1: Look! They're making a movie. What is it about?

ONLOOKER 2: Let's ask...
Excuse me, what's the movie about?

MAN 2: It's about India's independence in 1947.

ONLOOKER 1: Who's the man in the suit?

MAN 2: It's Nehru, India's first prime minister.

Track 77

WOMAN 1: Hey, you were going to be extras in a film! How did it go?

SANDRA: It was OK.

CARL: OK?! It was great! You're looking at the new movie stars. It was a film about the Roman Empire, you know, Julius Caesar and all that.

WOMAN 1: What did you do?

SANDRA: We got to the studios really early. First we got our costumes. Carl was a soldier ...

CARL: A gladiator!

SANDRA: OK, Carl was a gladiator and I was a Roman woman in the crowd. Then we went to the make-up department and we waited for hours until they put on our make-up.

WOMAN 1: What happened next?

SANDRA: Next they rehearsed, you know, practised, the gladiator scenes for a long time! Finally, they filmed a bit of the crowd. And that was it. After that we went home!

WOMAN 1: What about the gladiator scene?

CARL: Oh, there was no time to film that. But I did wear the costume all day!

Track 78

WOMAN: Who was Yuri Gagarin?

- What do you know about his career?
- Wow! What happened after that? Did he go round the Earth again?
- Oh no! That's sad.

Track 79

a The most comfortable way to see London is by taxi.
b You can take a boat from Westminster Pier.
c If you want to take a bus, look for a bus stop.
d You can park your car in the centre of London, but it's very expensive.
e Take a train to visit places outside London.
f You can ride a bike safely in a large guided group.
g The best way to see London is on foot.
h The first underground train is at 5.30 a.m.

Track 80

a CYNTHIA: And that was it. We had a really good time.
FRAN: Good. Listen, I have to go now. It was nice to talk to you.
CYNTHIA: Yes, see you soon, Fran.
FRAN: Yes, bye now.

b MARK: I had a great time.
SUE: Me too. Thank you!
MARK: Well, good night, Sue.
SUE: Good night, Mark.

c ROB: Hi Karen! How's it going?
KAREN: I can't talk now, Rob. Bye.
ROB: Oh, right. Bye then.

d DIANA: Hi Carmen. How was your holiday?
CARMEN: It was great!
DIANA: You must tell me all about it. I'll call you, OK?
CARMEN: OK. See you, Diana.
DIANA: Yes, goodbye!

Track 81

MAN: Hi! How's it going?

WOMAN: Fine, thanks. You?

MAN: Great. Did you have a good holiday?

WOMAN: Yes, we did. It was fun.

MAN: Well, I have to go. It was nice to talk to you.

WOMAN: You too. See you around.

MAN: Yes, bye.

Track 82

a WOMAN: Fine, thanks.
b WOMAN: Yes, thank you. Everybody's fine. What about your family?
c WOMAN: Nice to see you too. Let's get together some time.
d WOMAN: Yes, give me a call.
e WOMAN: Bye. See you soon.

Track 83

WOMAN: You know, people say there is treasure on this island.

MAN: Treasure? Don't be silly.

WOMAN: No, really. It's a box with lots of money.

MAN: And where is this treasure?

WOMAN: People say it's behind some rocks, near the forest at the bottom of a cliff. Look, here's a map of the island.

MAN: Near the forest, at the bottom of a cliff. Hey, look, there is a cave at the bottom of Western Cliffs, Goodluck Cave. Maybe it's there! Let's go and look for it!

WOMAN: Relax. I'm only joking.

MAN: Ha ha, very funny. But maybe it's true. Goodluck Cave. Good luck ...

Track 84

1 WOMAN: Where are you?
MAN: I'm lost.
WOMAN: What can you see?
MAN: Well, the sea, of course. I'm on a beach with lots of trees at the bottom of a cliff.

WOMAN: Are you near a cave?
MAN: Erm ... yes, I can see a cave near here.
WOMAN: OK. I know where you are. Don't move. I'm coming.

2 WOMAN: Where are you?
MAN: I'm lost.
WOMAN: What can you see?
MAN: Well, the sea, of course and a beach. I'm in a forest, near a river, on a mountain.
WOMAN: Are you near a village?
MAN: No, but I can see one far, far away.
WOMAN: OK. I know where you are. Don't move. I'm coming.

Track 85

1 MAN: Do you think you're going to get the job?
WOMAN: I hope so! I really want that job!

2 WOMAN 1: Do you think it's going to rain?
WOMAN 2: I hope not. We're having a party in the garden.

3 MAN 1: Are Liverpool going to win the Cup this year?
MAN 2: Well, they are the best team. Keep your fingers crossed!

4 WOMAN 1: So when are you getting married?
WOMAN 2: On 2nd May. I hope you can come!

5 WOMAN: Are you going to buy that new car?
MAN: Well, I hope that I have enough money.

Track 86

a I have a stomach ache.
b I have an English test tomorrow.
c Thank you very much for my present.
d We're going to visit your country!
e We're going to be there in July. Is it going to rain, do you think?
f Do you think we're going to like the food?

Track 87

a MAN: I'm going to see a movie.
WOMAN: Oh yeah? Which cinema are you going to?

b WOMAN: We're going to eat out. Do you want to come?
MAN: Great. I hear there's a fantastic new restaurant in town.

c MAN: We're going clubbing on Saturday.
WOMAN: Are you going to your usual club?

d WOMAN: Bob's taking the kids to see the Egyptian mummies.
MAN: Which museum are they going to?

e MAN: We're going to listen to the Symphony Orchestra!
WOMAN: How lovely! I love going to the concert hall.

f WOMAN: Are you going to the England v Germany match?
MAN: No, I'm not going to the stadium. I'm going to watch it on TV.

g MAN: I'm going to see a Shakespeare play tonight.
WOMAN: Are you? I haven't been to the theatre in years.

h WOMAN: Jill and Jim are going to a photograph exhibition.
MAN: Really? Which gallery are they going to?

Track 88

1
WILL: What are we going to do today, Tessa? Why don't we go to the cinema or something?
TESSA: Again? Let's go to an exhibition instead. There's a good one at Tate Modern.
WILL: What is it?
TESSA: Modern French painting.
WILL: That sounds interesting. Let's do that. We can have lunch at their cafeteria.
TESSA: An exhibition and lunch! What a great idea, Will!

2
MEERA: What shall we do on Saturday, Jake? Let's go to a museum, or a concert.
JAKE: Saturday? Well, the thing is, Meera, there's a football match on television.
MEERA: Oh what? Jake!
JAKE: Listen, why don't we watch the match on Saturday? And we can go to a concert on Sunday.
MEERA: Oh. OK, let's do that. And you can buy me dinner after the concert.
JAKE: Hmm, I suppose.

3
OLIVER: Anne? This is Oliver. What are your plans for Saturday night? I've got two tickets for the theatre. It's a musical. Do you want to come? And shall we go to that nice Italian restaurant afterwards? I hope you can make it! Call me.
ANNE: Oliver? I'd love to come. Where shall we meet? ...

Track 89

MAN: What shall we do on Saturday?
WOMAN: Why don't we go to the cinema?
MAN: Is there anything good on?
WOMAN: There's a Japanese film on at the local cinema.
MAN: That sounds interesting. Let's do that.
WOMAN: Shall I go and buy the tickets?
MAN: You don't have to go and buy the tickets. You can buy them on the phone.
WOMAN: That's a good idea.

Track 90

IRINA: Wow! It's the weekend, finally! What are you going to do tomorrow?
– That sounds good. What are your plans for Sunday?
– I'm going to go to a pop concert.
– Shall we talk again next week?
– Well, have a good weekend!

Track 91

a That boy is tall.
b This mountain is high.
c What a beautiful girl!
d This road is really narrow.
e Wow! What a thick book.
f That's a long river.
g That woman is really thin.
h That man is handsome.

Track 92

BENNY: Remember, Celia. We've got £560. Let's be careful.
CELIA: OK, dinner service first.
BENNY: Here's a nice one. It's only £80.
CELIA: Hmm. It isn't big enough. Now, this one is lovely.
BENNY: But it's much more expensive. Let's buy the smaller one. It's big enough for now.
CELIA: Oh, all right. Now, we need a toaster.
BENNY: We got two toasters for the wedding!
CELIA: Yes, but we need a bigger one. Look, like this one.
BENNY: That's £120! It's really too expensive.
CELIA: We can exchange the other two. Look, the ones we got are £40 each. So we only have to pay £40. Is that cheap enough?
BENNY: I suppose. Let's look at more exciting things now, like a DVD recorder.
CELIA: But we've got a DVD player. Isn't that good enough?
BENNY: No. A recorder is better than a player. It's reduced to only £200.
CELIA: OK. How much money have we got left?
BENNY: That's £80 for the dinner service, £40 for the toaster, £200 for the DVD player ... £320, we've got £240 left.
CELIA: Let's spend some of that on lunch. I'm starving.
BENNY: Good idea. What else is on the list? ...

Track 93

JESPER: Where shall we have the party, on the beach?
ELLA: No, it's too hot.
JESPER: In the house?
ELLA: The house isn't big enough.
JESPER: What about the garden then?
ELLA: Yes, the garden is better. It's large enough. And it's cooler than the beach.
JESPER: OK, the garden then. Shall we have Indian food?
ELLA: Oh no, it's too spicy.
JESPER: Italian?
ELLA: Hmm, too boring.
JESPER: How about a barbecue? Is that exciting enough?
ELLA: Yes, that sounds nice.
JESPER: Great, let's send the invitations.
ELLA: It's too soon. Let's wait a bit.

Track 94

MAN: What kind of movie do you want to see, a romantic comedy, a western or an action film?
– What time shall we go, at 2 p.m., 6 p.m. or 10 p.m.?
– Shall we go to a restaurant after?
– OK. Do you want to walk or take a taxi? Or shall we take our bikes?
– OK. See you later.

Track 95

a I have a Blackberry™. I use it all the time to phone and email people.
b We love our plasma screen TV. The picture is great.
c I've just bought a new digital camera – it takes great photos and you see them instantly.
d I can work anywhere now that I've got a new laptop computer.
e Where's my memory stick? I need to take it out of my camera to print some photos.
f I'm so glad we have a cordless phone, so that I can move around and do other things when I'm talking to people.
g Put the DVD recorder on – I want to record this TV programme.
h Have you seen our high definition TV? It's great!

Track 96

BETH: I read an article about some fantastic new technology. You know, robots that clean the house, that kind of thing. It sounds fun.
DAVE: I agree with you, Beth. It sounds fun, but not really important.
BETH: You're wrong. Anything that makes life better is important, don't you agree?
DAVE: Yes, you're right, but a robot is not going to make your life better, not really.
BETH: OK Dave. What new technology would you like to have, then?
DAVE: Maybe a machine to save the water you use in the house, for example.
BETH: What? The dirty water?
DAVE: Yes. All the water from the bath and kitchen can go to a special tank. The tank cleans the water and you can use it again and again. Now that's great technology!
BETH: Hmm. I don't agree with you. The same water all the time, yuck! And you can wash up tonight. You never do!
DAVE: That's wrong! I did it only the other day.

Track 97

a I think robots that clean the house are a really good idea. What do you think?
b Computers are better than people. They don't make mistakes, don't you agree?
c Big, fast cars in big cities are a really bad idea, don't you think?
d I think cycling is better than driving. Do you agree with me?
e Space travel doesn't do anything good for people.
f Listen to this in the paper: 'Computer games are bad for children'. Do you agree with that?

Answer key

Unit 1

A

1 Thank you!
That's OK.
Sorry!
See you later!
Bye!
Excuse me.
Sorry?
I don't understand.

2 a That's OK
b Sorry!
c see you later! Bye!
d Excuse me
e Sorry
f I don't understand

4 a Sorry!
b Thank you! That's OK.
c I don't understand.
d Excuse me!
e Sorry?

B

1 a Janie
b Steve
c Françoise
d Ms Peters
e Mr Watanabe

2 **Greeting**
Hello
Good morning
Hi
Introducing
I'm …
This is …
Responding
Nice to meet you
Pleased to meet you

3 a I'm
b Hi
c I'm
d this is
e Nice to meet you
f Nice to meet you
g Good morning
h This is
i Pleased to meet you
j Pleased to meet you

Unit 2

A

1 a France
b South Africa
c China
d Mexico
e Russia
f Korea

3 Canada – Sue
Brazil – Milton
Australia – Miranda
Japan – Ken
United Kingdom – Karen
USA – Ed

4 a 9
b 7
c 4
d 6
e 11
f 8
g 10
h 12
i 2
j 3
k 1
l 5

5 Brazilian
Korean
Russian
American
Australian
French
British
Chinese
Japanese
Mexican
South African
Canadian

B

1 a – Conversation 3
b – Conversation 2
c – Conversation 1

3 *Sample answer:*
a Hello!
Good morning!
How's it going?
Fine, thanks.
b Hello!
Good afternoon.
How are you?
Very well, thank you.
c Hello!
Good evening.
How are you?
Fine, thank you.
d Hi!
Hello!
How's it going?
Fine, thanks. You?

Unit 3

A

1 a actor
b taxi driver
c architect
d singer
e student
f cleaner
g nurse
h teacher
i doctor
j engineer
k accountant
l cook

2 a accountant, architect
b cook
c student, teacher
d actor, singer
e cleaner, nurse, doctor
f taxi driver

3 a He works in a theatre. He is an actor.
b He works in the street. He is a taxi driver.
c She works in an office. She is an architect.
d She works in a theatre. She is a singer.
e He works in a school. He is a student.
f She works in a school / office / hospital. She is a cleaner.
g She is a nurse. She works in a hospital / school.
h He is a teacher. He works in a school.
i She is a doctor. She works in a hospital.
j He is an engineer. He works in the street.
k She is an accountant. She works in an office.
l He is a cook. He works in a kitchen.

B

1 Linda – nurse
Marshall – actor
Marie – cook
Richard – cleaner

2 **Asking about jobs**
What's your job?
What do you do?
Answering
I'm a(n) …
Reacting
Oh, really?
That's great.
That's interesting.

Unit 4

A

1 a brothers
b sisters
c husband, wife
d cousins
e mother, father
f sons, daughters
g grandmother, grandchildren
h uncle, aunt

B

1 1, 2, 3, 4, 5, 6, 7, 8, 9, 10, 11, 12, 13, 14, 15, 16, 17, 18, 19, 20, 30, 40, 50, 60, 70, 80, 90, 100

2 twenty-six
thirty-one
forty-five
sixty-nine
seventy-seven
eighty-three
eighty-nine
ninety-four

3 a – Conversation 4
b – Conversation 1
c – Conversation 3
d – Conversation 2

4 a 2 b 3 c 1

5 a How, is
She's X years
b *student's own answer*
c How, are
a few days old
d How old are
student's own answer
e How old is Daniel?
He's XX years old.

Unit 5

A

a have breakfast
b have a shower
c relax
d go to bed
e go to work
f get up
g read the paper
h watch television
i sleep
j work

3 *student's own answer*

B

1 a 3 b 1 c 4 d 2

2 a What time is it now?
b What time is your class?
c 12
d three
e half past twelve

3 a What time is it in San Francisco?
b What's the time in Mexico City?
c What time is it in Paris?
d What time is it in Sydney?
e What's the time in São Paulo?
f What time is it in your country?

4 a It's four o'clock in the morning.
b It's quarter past nine in the morning.
c It's quarter to ten in the morning.
d It's half past eight in the evening.
e It's three minutes past eleven in the morning.
f *student's own answer*

Unit 6

A

1 *student's own answer*

2 a do
b like, how about

3 a cake
b chicken
c soda
d crisps
e eggs
f fish

4 *Sample answer:*
a We have a big lunch and a small meal in the evening.
b I also have fruit or fruit juice.
c I have meat or fish with vegetables or a salad.
d We have cheese or eggs, and fruit.
e I like chocolate or sweets too.

B

1

1 cheese sandwich, a cup of tea
£6.25

2 fish and chips, Coke
£5.50

2 a What would you like to drink?
b Can I help you?
c Anything else?
d I'll have a cup of tea.
e I'd like fish and chips.
f Can I have some ketchup, please?

3 a I'd like a cheese sandwich and a chocolate ice cream, please.
b I'll have a cup of coffee. Milk, no sugar.
c No thank you.

Unit 7

A

1 a travelling
b Martin
c watching TV
d Chloe
e reading
f Candy
g going to the cinema
h Marie and John
i listening to music
j Sally and Karen

2 **I like playing …**
football
basketball
volleyball
tennis
baseball
golf
I like going …
running
swimming
skiing
skateboarding

3 a Jane likes playing football.
b Jane likes going to the cinema.
c Marie likes playing golf.
d Marie likes listening to music.
e Kevin and Trudy like going swimming.
f Kevin and Trudy like reading.

B

1 a disagree
b agree
c disagree
d agree
e disagree

2 a I agree.
b Of course.

c I don't think so.
d That's not right.
e Certainly not.
3 1 b 2 a 3 d 4 c
4 *student's own answer*

Unit 8

A

1 a head
b eye
c tooth
d hand
e stomach
f leg
g foot
h back
i chest
j arm
k throat
l mouth
m nose
n ear
2 a head
b legs, feet
c mouth / throat / chest
d back
e mouth / stomach
f nose
g eyes, ears
h mouth, teeth
i chest / nose
j arms, legs / feet
3 **Eat**
mouth
hands
stomach
Play football
legs
feet
Use a computer
hands
eyes
Work out
arms
legs
stomach
Listen to an MP3 player
ears

B

1 a 3 b 5 c 2 d 4 e 1
2 Conversation 1: c, g, k
Conversation 2: d, j, n
Conversation 3: e, i, m
Conversation 4: b, f, l
Conversation 5: a, h, o
3 a What's the matter with Janie?
Her throat hurts.
Poor Janie.
b What's wrong with Billy?
He's got a problem.
Oh, dear. Poor Billy.
c How do you feel?
I feel awful. My head hurts.
You poor thing!

Unit 9

A

1 a dress
b suit
c trousers
d shirt
e shoes
f tie
g skirt
h T-shirt
i sweater
j jacket
k socks
2 *student's own answer*
3 a dress
jacket
shirt
skirt
suit
sweater
tie
T-shirt
a pair of
shoes
socks
trousers
4 a shoes
b suit, tie
c trousers
d dress
e skirt
f shirt, jacket
g T-shirts

B

1 1 skirt
2 medium
3 try
4 tie
5 this
6 does it
7 it
2 a like
b medium
c much
d does
e cost
f about
g want
h take
3 **Customer**
c, d, e, g, h, j
Assistant
a, b, f, i
4 1 Excuse me. How much is this bread?
It's £1.50 a loaf.
I'll take two, please. How much is that?
That's £3.00. Anything else?
No, thank you.
2 I'd like a dress.
Certainly. What about this black one?
How much does it cost?
£50. Do you want to try it?
Yes, please.

Unit 10

A

1 100% – always
80% – usually
60–80% – often
40–50% – sometimes
10–20% – occasionally
0% – never
2 *student's own answer*
3 a throw a ball
b hit a ball
c ride a horse / bicycle / motorbike
d drive a car
e climb a tree / mountain
4 a drive
b ride
c ride
d climb
e dance

B

1 four times
2 a Can you speak slowly, please?
b does 'welfare' mean?
c Can you say that again,
d do you say
3 a 3 b 1 c 4 d 2
4 a Do you want to come to the cinema with us?
b Can you speak more slowly, please?
c There's a great movie this evening.
d What does 'movie' mean?
e It's a film.
f Can you say that again, please?
g A movie is a film at the cinema.
h I'd love to go to the movie!

Unit 11

A

1 a short
  b thin, slim, medium build, overweight, chubby
  c medium length, long
  d blonde, grey, red, dark
  e straight, wavy, curly
  f brown, green, black, blue

3 a Larry
  b Helen

4 *Sample answer:*
Alicia is tall and slim. She's got short curly black hair and brown eyes.
Frank is slim and medium height. He's got short, straight red hair

B

1 Simone

2 a How old is she?
  b What does she look like?
  c How tall is she?
  d How much does she weigh?

3 1 e 2 d 3 b 4 a 5 c

4 a Do you know Maxine?
  b She's got black hair and brown eyes.
  c Five foot five.
  d About 125 pounds.
  e She's 21.

Unit 12

A

1 *student's own answer*

2 Sherry talks on the phone for hours!
Tom likes playing games on the computer.
Leave Mike a message on his answering machine.
Find the information on the Internet.
Call me on my mobile phone.
Jane always sends her reports by fax.
I often send photos by email.
We sometimes order food by phone.

3 *Sample answer:*
I leave voice messages on an answering machine.
I use the computer or my mobile phone to send emails.
I also use the computer to play games.
I use the phone to make phone calls.
I use my mobile phone to make phone calls, send text messages, take and send photos and go on the Internet.

4 a leave
  b play
  c make
  d send
  e go
  f take
  g send

5 Ron is making a phone call.
Mike is sending an email.
Alice is playing a game on the computer.
Charlie is taking photos on his camera.

B

1 a two
  b No, because she doesn't want to.
  c No, because she's at the cinema.

2 a This is Robin.
  b Do you want to leave a message?
  c Who's speaking?
  d Can I take a message?

3 a Hello.
  b speak to
  c Who's speaking
  d It's
  e leave a message
  f Thanks, Bye
  g Bye

5 **Message for:**
Lyndsay
Message taken by:
Fernando
Message:
Mariana and Robin aren't coming to the party, because Robin is sick.

Unit 13

A

1

S	O	F	A	C	B	E	G	D	I	R	F
T	S	G	H	I	O	K	J	E	F	E	R
O	W	Y	I	U	N	H	Y	S	Q	W	K
V	D	T	Z	X	P	B	N	K	M	O	E
E	W	A	Y	G	I	P	M	F	V	H	C
D	B	B	C	U	R	T	A	I	N	S	M
Q	R	L	I	R	P	L	D	L	A	M	P
H	J	E	K	M	N	B	R	S	E	T	U
K	O	P	L	T	E	L	I	O	T	E	P
S	Y	B	E	D	W	B	A	M	N	K	B
X	P	A	H	M	L	U	H	Y	T	R	S
R	E	T	U	P	M	O	C	I	V	Q	D

2 a TV
  b fridge
  c lamp
  d table
  e bed
  f stove
  g sofa
  h rug
  i chair
  j shower
  k desk
  l toilet
  m computer
  n curtains

3 *Sample answer:*
Bathroom
toilet
shower
Kitchen
stove
fridge
Dining room
table
chairs
rug
curtains
Living room
sofa
chairs
lamp
TV
rug
curtains
Bedroom
bed
desk
computer
chair
curtains

B

1 a 2 b 1 c 2 d 2
2 a Have you seen
  b I don't know
  c Is it
  d It's on
  e Here it is
  f There
3 **Conversation 1**
  Have you seen my watch?
  No. Is it under the newspaper?
  Where's the newspaper?
  In the living room.
  No, it isn't under the newspaper.
  Is it in the bathroom?
  Oh, yes. Here it is.
  Conversation 2
  Where are my glasses?
  Are they on the fridge?
  No, they aren't in the kitchen.
  Are they in the living room?
  Oh yes, here they are, next to the TV.
4 a Are they on the table?
  b Are they under the book?
  c Are they next to the door?

Unit 14

A

1 a 8 b 3 c 7 d 6 e 10 f 12 g 5 h 1 i 2 j 9 k 11 l 4 m 13 n 14
2 **Across**
  2 supermarket
  4 cinema
  7 hospital
  8 library
  10 post office
  Down
  1 park
  2 swimming pool
  3 town hall
  5 bank
  6 gym
  9 school

B

1 library: on the right of the map
  supermarket: on the left of the map
  sports centre: at the top of the map
2 a Is there
  b right
  c your right
  d your left
  e left
3 a where's
    up, on the right
  b is there
    along, turn, on the right
  c where's
    up, turn, go, hospital, the left
  d is there, near here
    Go, turn, on the right
4 is there
  Go straight along, left, go up, on the left
5 a Go along Park Street. The library is on your right.
  b Yes, go straight along Park Street. Turn right into High Street and the supermarket is on your right.
  c Here, in Park Street, on your right.
  d Go straight along Park Street. Turn right into High Street and the town hall is on your left.

Unit 15

A

1 1 e – piano
  2 g – guitar
  3 d – violin
  4 b – trumpet
  5 c – drums
  6 f – saxophone
  7 a – clarinet
2 Mozart – classical
  Coldplay – pop
  Louis Armstrong – jazz
  Johnny Cash – country
  Anastacia – dance
  Eminem – hip-hop
3 *student's own answer*
4 a violin, piano
  b rock, guitar
  c guitar, drums, guitar, piano
  d jazz, trumpet

B

1 a 4 b 3 c 1 d 2
2 1 May I
  2 Can I
  3 Can I
  4 Do you mind if I
4 a May I turn the music down?
  b Do you mind if I open the window?
  c Can I go to Joe's party tonight?
  d Do you mind if I watch the TV?
  e Can I borrow your car?
  f Can I listen to your CDs?
5 1 b 2 f 3 e 4 a 5 d 6 c

Unit 16

A

1 a art
  b biology
  c geography
  d chemistry
  e physical education (PE)
  f history
  g English
  h physics
  i mathematics (maths)
2 easy
  interesting
  history, English, art, biology
  boring
  PE
  difficult
  interesting
  maths, chemistry
  boring
  physics, geography
3 *Student's own answer*

B

1 English textbook d
  money a
  MP3 player b
  pencil c
2 1 d 2 c 3 a 4 b
3 1 d 2 c 3 a 4 b
4 a lend
  b borrow
  c borrow
  d lend
5 1 c 2 d 3 a 4 b

Unit 17

A

1 a cat
  b dog
  c rabbit
  d mouse
  e lion
  f tiger
  g rat
  h horse
  i kangaroo
  j giraffe
  k rhinoceros
  l elephant
2 giraffe
  mouse
  rabbit
  cat
  dog
  rhinoceros
  rat
  kangaroo
  horse
  elephant
3 a lion
  b kangaroos
  c cats, dogs
  d rabbits
  e elephants
  f giraffe

B

1 a 3 b 2 c 1 d 4
2 1 Be, don't
 2 Look
 3 Mind
 4 Don't
3 Keep 1 b
 Mind 2 d
 Look 3 c
 Don't 4 a
4 *Sample answer:*
 a Look out! It's fragile.
 b Don't walk on the grass.
 c Be careful! There's a mouse under the table.
 d Don't walk on the dog.
6 *Sample answer:*
 a Look out! There is some water.
 Mind the water!
 Don't walk in the water!
 Be careful! There is some water.
 b Look out! There's a rat.
 Be careful! There's a rat.
 c Don't touch that dog!
 Mind the dog!
 d Don't sit on the glasses!
 Mind the glasses!
 Look out! There are some glasses.
 Be careful! There are some glasses.

Unit 18

A

1 1 rain
 2 sun
 3 ice
 4 clouds
 5 wind
 6 snow
2 a 1 b 2 c 4 d 2 e 3, 6 f 6 g 5 h 3 i 2
4 a It's windy and it's raining.
 b It's hot and sunny.
 c It's cold, snowing and icy.
5 1 summer
 2 spring
 3 winter
 4 autumn

B

1 d, g, e, h, b, a, f, c
2 a great
 b lovely
 c love
 d awful
 e hate
3 *student's own answer*
4 a 4 b 1 c 2 d 3
5 *Sample answer:*
 a I don't. I hate watching TV.
 b No, I don't. It's awful.
 c Yes, I love the rain.
 d No, I hate hot weather.

Unit 19

A

1 1789 a
 1947 f
 2006 g
 1865 e
 1861 d
 1509 b
 1547 c
2 a 1861 to 1865
 b 1789
 c 1509 to 1547
 d 1947
3 1 a 2 b, c 3 b, c 4 a 5 d 6 a
4 a nineteen fourteen
 b nineteen forty-five
 c nineteen forty-seven
 d nineteen fifty-two
 e nineteen sixty-three
5 a queen, 1952
 b Prime Minister, 1947
 c War, 1914
 d Word, 1945
 e 1963, President

B

1 c, a, b, d
2 a What happened next?
 b Then
 c Next
 d Finally
3 b First
 e Next
 d Then
 c After that
 a Finally
4 *Sample answer:*
 Yuri Gagarin was from Russia. He was the world's first cosmonaut. These are some important events in his life. First, he worked in a steel factory. Next, he took flying lessons as a hobby. Then, he became a pilot in the Russian airforce. After that, he trained to become a cosmonaut. Finally, Yuri flew around the Earth. The flight took only 1 hour and 48 minutes. Yuri Gagarin died in 1968 when his plane crashed.
5 *Sample answer:*
 a He was the world's first cosmonaut.
 b First, he worked in a steel factory. Next, he took flying lessons as a hobby. Then, he became a pilot in the Russian airforce. After that, he trained to become a cosmonaut. Finally, Yuri flew around the Earth. The flight took only 1 hour and 48 minutes.
 c No. He died in 1968 when his plane crashed.

Unit 20

A

1 a taxi
 b boat
 c bus
 d car
 e train
 f bike
 g on foot
 h underground
2 By underground h
 By bus c
 By train e
 By taxi a
 By boat b
 By car d
 By bike f
 On foot g
3 a At a bus stop.
 b Westminster Pier.
 c Railway stations.
 d 5.30 a.m.
 e In a bicycle lane, or with a large guided group.
 f By bus (from the top of a double-decker).
 g In a car park (but it's expensive).
 h By taxi.

4

C	O	N	V	E	R	T	I	B	L	E
A	B	I	C	D	E	I	F	G	H	M
R	I	A	J	K	L	C	M	N	R	O
A	O	R	P	B	I	K	E	Q	I	T
V	R	T	S	U	T	E	U	V	D	O
A	W	X	Y	S	Z	T	U	B	E	R
N	A	E	I	O	U	P	L	A	N	H
J	D	R	I	V	E	A	V	I	M	O
I	K	E	C	A	F	L	E	P	A	M
S	P	A	A	L	L	P	L	A	N	E
F	O	U	R	B	Y	F	O	U	R	E

a convertible, bike, tube, plane, four by four, caravan, train, car, motor home
b drive, fly, ride
c map, ticket

B

1 **a** have to go now
was nice to talk to you
see you soon
bye now
b good night
Good night
c Bye
Bye then
d See you
goodbye

2 b, d, e, g, a, c, f

3 *Sample answer:*
a Hi! How's it going?
b Is your family well?
c Everybody's fine, thanks. Listen I have to go now. It was nice to see you.
d Great. I'll call you.
e Bye for now.

Unit 21

A

1 Blue Rock Mountains
Western Cliffs
Goodluck Cave
Black Forest
La Joya Village
Arenas River
Paradise Beach
Shark Beach

2 Goodluck Cave, in the bottom left-hand corner of the map

3 **a** 1 **b** 2

B

1 a I hope she comes!
2 1 b 2 e 3 a 4 c 5 d
3 a I hope not
  b I hope
  c I hope
  d I hope not
  e I hope so
4 a 3 b 4 c 2 d 1
5 *Sample answer:*
  a I hope you feel better soon.
  b I hope it goes well for you.
  c I hope you like it.
  d I hope you can come and see us.
  e I hope not. We want to go to the beach.
  f I hope so. French food is very nice.

Unit 22

A

1 a theatre
  b stadium
  c gallery
  d museum
  e restaurant
  f concert hall
  g club
  h cinema
2 a cinema
  b restaurant
  c club
  d museum
  e concert hall
  f stadium
  g theatre
  h gallery
3 *Sample answer:*
  a I want to go to the cinema to see/watch a film.
  b I want to go to a gallery to see some photographs.
  c I want to go to the theatre to see a play.
  d I want to go to the stadium to see/watch a match.
  e I want to go to a restaurant to have a meal.
  f I want to go to the museum to see an exhibition.
  g I want to go to the concert hall to listen to a famous pianist.

B

1 Tessa and Will are going to an exhibition and a cafeteria today. Jake and Meera are going to stay at home on Saturday; they are going to a concert and a restaurant on Sunday. Anne and Oliver are going to the theatre and to a restaurant on Saturday.
2 a Will
  b Meera
  c Oliver
  d Will
  e Tessa
  f Jake
  g Oliver
  h Oliver
  i Will
  j Will
  k Tessa
  l Jake
  m Anne
3 1 What shall we do on Saturday?
  2 Why don't we go to the cinema?
  3 Is there anything good on?
  4 There's a Japanese film on at the local cinema.
  5 That sounds interesting. Let's do that.
  6 Shall I go and buy the tickets?
  7 You don't have to go and buy the tickets. You can buy them on the phone.
  8 That's a good idea.
4 *Sample answer:*
  a I'm going to the theatre.
  b I'm going to stay at home.
  c That sounds good.
  d OK, I'll call you.
  e Thank you, you too.

Unit 23

A

1 a tall
  b high
  c beautiful
  d narrow
  e thick
  f long
  g thin
  h handsome
2 a plain
  b cheap
  c unattractive
  d low
  e short
  f old-fashioned
  g wide
  h short
  i thin
  j thick, fat

  1 wide
  2 cheap
  3 fat
  4 old-fashioned
  5 plain
  6 low
  7 unattractive
  8 thin
  9 short
  10 short
3 a cheap
  b old-fashioned
  c unattractive
  d wide
  e plain
  f low
  g fat
4 a low
  b tall, attractive
  c high, beautiful
  d old-fashioned, short, long
  e beautiful, attractive

B

1 a dinner service
  b dinner service
  c toaster
  d toaster
  e DVD player
  f dinner service
  g dinner service
  h toaster
  i DVD recorder
  j DVD recorder
2 a The coffee is too sweet.
  b The flat is too small.
  c The jacket isn't big enough.
  d The shoes are too expensive.
  e The film is too long.
  f The caravan is too high.
  g The boy isn't tall enough.
3 a It's too hot.
  b It isn't big enough. It's too small.
  c It's better. It's large enough and it's cooler.
  d It's too spicy.
  e It's not exciting enough. It's too boring.
  f It's better. It's exciting enough.
  g It's too soon.
  They are going to have the party in the garden and they are going to have a barbecue.
4 *student's own answer*

Unit 24

A

1 a 4 b 3 c 1 d 2 e 2 f 4 g 3 h 3
2 a Eyesee
  b Sonic recorder
  c Nomad
  d Sonic recorder
  e Nomad
  f Robbie

g Eyesee
h Nomad
i Eyesee

3 a digital camera
b plasma screen
c laptop computer
d cordless phone
e Blackberry™
f DVD recorder
g memory stick
h high definition television

4 a digital camera
b plasma screen, high definition television
c laptop computer, Blackberry™
d laptop computer
e memory stick
f cordless phone

B

1 a Beth
b Dave
c Beth
d Dave

2 a don't you agree
b I agree with you
c You're right
d You're wrong
e I don't agree with you

3 a 4 b 2 c 1 d 5 e 3

4 *student's own answer*

Notes